KU-659-172

The £5 feast

Edited by Gail Duff

Gail Duff began her career in broadcasting on BBC Radio Medway talking about cooking. She taught herself to cook, and is particularly interested in the art of using fresh seasonal food to its best advantage. She has since broadcast on national radio and has had two television series on BBC1's *Pebble Mill at One.* She is a regular contributor to Radio 4's *Woman's Hour.* Gail also writes for *Good Housekeeping, Parents, Daily Telegraph, Living* and *The Food Magazine,* and has published a number of cookery books. *Fresh all the Year,* a particular success in both hardback and paperback editions, was the first of several to promote the values of good country cooking.

Gail lives with her husband and baby daughter in the countryside near Maidstone. Her large garden provides many of the ingredients she uses in her cooking.

THE £5 FEAST

'WOMAN'S HOUR' COMPETITION RECIPES
EDITED BY GAIL DUFF

ARIEL BOOKS
BRITISH BROADCASTING CORPORATION

Drawings by Ray and Corinne Burrows

© British Broadcasting Corporation 1983

First published 1983

Published by the British Broadcasting Corporation
35 Marylebone High Street London W1M 4AA

Typeset by Phoenix Photosetting, Chatham

Printed in England by Mackays of Chatham Ltd

ISBN 0 563 20162 2

Contents

Introduction

This book grew naturally from a series of broadcasts that I did for *Woman's Hour* in the spring of 1982 called 'Food on the Cheap'. Basically, it was about how to use cheap ingredients to their best advantage in order to produce imaginative and interesting meals. It occured to me and to my producer, Pat Taylor, that there must be a good many housewives up and down the country who are very well used to cooking just such meals for their families nearly every day of their lives. What a good idea it would be if we could give them the opportunity to show off their talents. We therefore decided to run a competition for them. The rules were simple: plan a dinner party menu for four people, using original recipes, that would, at that time, cost under five pounds; write out the recipes and give a breakdown of costings.

The entries came in slowly at first, but by the time the series came to an end we had a hundred and fifty. I staggered home with them in two carrier bags and sat down to sort them out. Right from the start, I was really impressed. Like a school teacher, I rated them first on a scale from A to D. Over fifty per cent were 'A's, most to the rest were 'B's, with only one or two 'C's and no 'D's at all. It was good to discover that we have so many talented cooks in Britain. I nearly considered offering some of them a job!

The entrants came from all over the country, from Somerset to Yorkshire, from Scotland and Wales. The oldest competitor was aged seventy-nine; a mother and daughter had competed against each other and entered separate menus; and I was glad to see that two men had entered, one on his own and the other in a joint effort with his wife. There were also fourteen vegetarians.

We had many letters to say how much the entrants had enjoyed compiling their menus. One lady said that it had made her husband realise that menu planning was 'an intellectual exercise'; and many more said that as they had anything up to five children to feed every day, they were well used to careful budgeting. We were even told that we were extravagant by one lady who considered five pounds far too much to spend on one meal!

On reading through the menus, I was struck by the ingenuity that had gone into compiling them. People were making their own yoghurts, cheeses and breads. They were shopping around for bargains and most used fresh, seasonal produce to its best advantage. It was this seasonal aspect that probably influenced the fact that the two most used ingredients were watercress and lemons, both of which would be readily available in the spring, which was when the competition took place. Broccoli was one of the favourite vegetables also, I suspect for the same reason.

Our favourite meat, true to British country tradition, turned out to be pork, and it was good to see all the cheaper cuts being used, such as knuckle, shoulder and even pig's head. One lady wrote: 'Ask your butcher for a yard of pork. When I was a girl, one yard meant three feet'. She then gave a delicious recipe using three pig's trotters!

There was a good use of regional specialities and we had an oatmeal soup from Scotland and a dish of Torbay Sole from a lady in the West Country. One contributor used a 'free' rabbit, shot by a member of her family and that, together with her home-grown vegetables, enabled her to produce the cheapest menu, costing her only £1.08.

Some entrants even managed to include drinks in their costings. There were not as many making home-made wine as I had expected, but with one meal there was beer made from a Budget Bitter Kit, working out at £2.30 for 40 pints. Cider was popular, and several people purchased this from a local cider farm. China tea was a very good idea, but I did not really care for 'iced water served in an old Perrier bottle'! Coffee was occasionally included at the end of the meal and several menus included cheese and biscuits in addition to the sweet.

The over-all standard of entries was excellent, so how did I go about sorting out the winners? Besides choosing the most delicious recipes, I was also looking for well-balanced meals, both in terms of nutrition and in flavour and texture. Appearance can affect enjoyment of food, too, so a meal with a range of colourful dishes was also rated highly.

There were several menus where the main dish was excellent but was accompanied by a rather mediocre first course and sweet; and occasionally the same fault occurred the other way about. There were also cases where individual recipes would have been good alone, but all were rather the same in texture and flavour, or used similar ingredients, so not adding enough variety to the whole meal.

I believe that vegetables should always be included in a meal and so, too, did many of the top twenty-five entrants. Those who did not make that list often gave really good recipes for the three courses, but omitted either a cooked vegetable or a salad.

Something else that I noticed as I read through was presentation. Lists of all the ingredients, plus clear recipe instructions and detailed costings were what impressed me most.

With these points in mind, I chose the best twenty-five menus. Then the eventual winners of the competition were chosen with great difficulty by Mary Berry and myself. We had a long discussion one afternoon and in the end totally agreed with one another. Our top five menus scored on all counts. They were colourful, interesting, nutritious and delicious, with carefully worked out costings, coming easily within the five pound limit.

The recipes in all the final twenty-five menus were so good that it seemed a pity to just leave them somewhere in a BBC file, when there must be many listeners eager to read them and try them out. So we compiled this book.

The winning menus are printed here in their entirety, but the others have been split into their separate courses so that you can mix and match to your own taste.

Mary and I certainly enjoyed judging the competition, and the entrants had a good time preparing the menus. Now everyone can join in *The Five Pound Feast*.

Gail Duff

Editor's note

The ingredients in the following recipes are exactly as given by the contributors. In some cases the wording has been changed slightly or additional explanatory notes have been added in order to maintain a uniform, easily comprehensible style throughout the book.

The recipes have not been tested by the editor, who cannot accept responsibility for their success or otherwise.

Unless otherwise stated, all the recipes will serve four people and all spoon measurements used are level.

The winning menus

First prize winner

Mrs L. K. Stoneley, Pulbrough, W. Sussex.

Tomato soup with curd cheese
and herbs
Home-made wholemeal rolls

———————— ❧ ————————

Crispy pork parcels with cider sauce
Savoury rice

———————— ❧ ————————

Blackberry and Applemint
yoghurt ice
Boudoir fingers

1 litre cider to drink included in cost
Cost, spring 1982: £4.75½

Tomato soup with curd cheese and herbs

1½ lb (675 g) tomatoes
2 oz (50 g) butter
1 medium onion, finely chopped
1½ pints (850 ml) chicken stock
½ oz (15 g) soft brown sugar
Salt and pepper
½ oz (15 g) flour
2–3 oz (50–75 g) curd cheese (see below)
1 tablespoon (15 ml) chopped fresh marjoram
1 tablespoon (15 ml) chopped fresh parsley
Salt

Halve and seed tomatoes. Rub the seeds in a sieve to extract the juice. Melt the butter in a saucepan on a low heat. Put in the onion and cook it until it is soft but not coloured. Add the tomatoes and their juice, stock, sugar and seasoning. Bring them to the boil and simmer the soup, covered, for 30–40 minutes so the tomatoes are soft and breaking up. Rub the contents of the pan through a sieve and discard the skins. Slake the flour with about 6 tablespoons (90 ml) of the soup. Stir it into the rest. Return the soup to the saucepan, bring it to the boil, stirring, and simmer until it is thick. Adjust the seasoning.

While the soup is cooking, cream the cheese in a bowl and beat in the herbs and a little salt.

To serve, pour into bowls and float a little cheese on top.

To make the curd cheese

Mix together 6 tablespoons (90 ml) skimmed milk powder, 1 tablespoon (215 ml) natural yoghurt and enough water at a temperature of 112–113F (50–55C) to make up 1 pint (575 ml). Pour the mixture into a wide-necked vacuum flask with a stopper, cover it and leave it undisturbed for 24 hours.

Pour this 'over-mature' yoghurt into a muslin bag and leave it to drip for 6 hours. The curd cheese will be left in the muslin.

Editor's note: If you do not wish to make your own curd cheese, it can be bought at most large supermarkets. Soften it with 1 tablespoon (15 ml) milk per 1 oz (25 g).

Crispy pork parcels

pancakes

4 oz (125 g) flour

Pinch salt

1 egg

½ pint (275 ml) milk

1 tablespoon (15 ml) oil

Oil for frying

filling

1 pork knuckle

1 tablespoon (15 ml) oil

1 lb (450 g) leeks, thinly sliced

Salt and pepper

2 cooking apples

½ oz (15 g) soft brown sugar

4 tablespoons (60 ml) water

¼ teaspoon (1.5 ml) ground cinnamon

5 cloves

3 sprigs fennel (if available)

finishing

1 egg yolk, beaten, or, flour and water paste

First make the pancakes. Sift the flour and salt into a bowl and make a well in the centre. Beat in the egg, half the milk, the oil and finally the remaining milk. Beat until you have a smooth batter and leave it in a cool place for 30 minutes. Make 8 pancakes with the batter by frying about 3 tablespoons (45 ml) at a time in hot oil on one side only. Remove and cool them.

Cut all the meat from the pork knuckle. There should be about 14 oz (400 g). Cut it into short, thin strips, across the grain of the meat. Heat the oil in a large frying pan on a high heat. Put in the pork and stir it until it begins to brown. Mix in the leeks, lower the heat, season and cook for 3 minutes, stirring, so the pork is cooked through and the leeks are beginning to soften.

Take the pan from the heat. Turn out the pork and cool it.

Peel, core and chop the apples. Put them into a saucepan with the water, sugar, cinnamon, cloves and fennel. Cover them and set them on a low heat for 15 minutes or until they are soft and can be beaten to a purée. Remove the cloves and fennel. Cool the purée and mix it into the pork and leeks.

Lay the pancakes cooked side up. Place a portion of the filling at one end of each pancake. Fold over the end, then the two sides, and then roll up the pancake to make a parcel. Seal the edges with egg yolk or flour and water paste.

Deep fry the parcels in hot oil for about 1 minute so they are crisp and golden.

Cider sauce

½ pint (275 ml) stock
½ pint (275 ml) cider
1 tablespoon (15 ml) arrowroot

Pour the stock and the cider into a saucepan and bring them to the boil. In a bowl, mix about ¼ pint (150 ml) of the hot liquid with the arrowroot. Stir the mixture back into the saucepan and simmer the sauce, stirring, until it thickens.

Serve separately in a jug to pour over the pork parcels.

Savoury rice

8 oz (225 g) long grain brown rice
1 red pepper, diced
8 oz (225 g) carrots, diced
8 oz (225 g) shelled peas, fresh or frozen

Put the rice into a saucepan with 1 pint (575 ml) lightly-salted water. Bring them to the boil. Add the vegetables, cover and cook on a low heat for 45 minutes or until the rice is tender and all the water has been absorbed.

Blackberry and applemint yoghurt water ice

One 10 oz (300 g) tin blackberries
1 pint (575 ml) home-made yoghurt (see below)
2 tablespoons (30 ml) chopped applemint
1 egg white
1 oz (25 g) icing sugar

Drain the blackberries, reserving the syrup. Rub the blackberries through a sieve. Mix the resulting purée into the yoghurt, adding 6 tablespoons (90 ml) of the syrup from the tin. Stir in the applemint. Freeze the mixture, stirring it about once an hour.

Stiffly whisk the egg white and whisk in the icing sugar. When the yoghurt mixture is almost frozen, turn it into a bowl and fold in the egg white. Freeze the mixture completely.

Yoghurt
Mix together 6 tablespoons (90 ml) skimmed milk powder, 1 tablespoon (15 ml) natural yoghurt and enough water at 112–113F (50–55C) to make it up to 1 pint (575 ml). Pour into a wide-necked vacuum flask and leave undisturbed for five hours.

Editor's notes 1. Bought yoghurt may be used instead of home-made. 2. Applemint is a variety of mint with a slight apple flavour. If it is not available, ordinary garden mint may be used instead.

Second prize winner*

Mrs Pam Lumsden, Keith, Banffshire.

Cream of carrot soup
Melba toast with butter curls

Pork chops in orange sauce
Braised celery
Broccoli or spring cabbage
Potatoes cooked with onions and milk

Caramelised apples

Cost, spring 1982: £4.81½
*Mrs Lumsden's menu is shown on the cover

Cream of carrot soup

1 lb (450 g) carrots
8 oz (225 g) tomatoes
3 oz (75 g) butter
1½ pints (850 ml) chicken stock, heated
Salt and pepper
½ pint (275 ml) milk, heated
2 tablespoons (30 ml) chopped parsley

Thinly slice the carrots. Scald, skin and chop the tomatoes. Melt the butter in a heavy saucepan on a low heat. Mix in the carrots and cook them gently for 3 minutes. Add the tomatoes and cook for 2 minutes more. Pour in the heated stock, bring to the boil and season. Simmer, covered, for about 45 minutes or until the carrots are soft.

Cool the soup slightly and liquidise it. Return it to the cleaned pan, add the hot milk and check the seasoning. Reheat gently, without boiling.

Pour the soup into individual bowls and scatter the parsley over the top. Serve with melba toast and butter curls.

Pork chops in orange sauce

4 pork chops
1 garlic clove
Salt and freshly-ground black pepper
2 medium oranges
2 oz (50 g) margarine
1 dessertspoon (10 ml) cornflour
8 fl oz (225 ml) stock
Squeeze of lemon juice
½ teaspoon (2.5 ml) chopped rosemary
1 bunch watercress

Heat the oven to 350F (180C) gas 4. Rub the chops with the cut garlic clove and sprinkle them with pepper. Reserve the garlic.

Squeeze the juice from 1½ oranges. Cut the rind and pith from the remaining half orange and cut the flesh into four slices.

Melt the margarine in a frying pan on a high heat. Put in the chops, brown them on both sides and remove them to a shallow ovenproof dish. Put an orange slice on each chop.

Lower the heat under the pan. Stir the cornflour into the pan juices to make a roux. Stir in the stock and orange and lemon juices. Bring them gently to the boil, stirring, and stir on a low heat until you have a thick sauce. Season and add the rosemary. If liked, chop and add the garlic clove. Pour the sauce over the chops. Put the chops into the oven for 1–1¼ hours.

Serve from the dish, garnished with watercress

Potatoes cooked with onion and milk

2 lb (900 g) potatoes
1 small onion
½ pint (275 ml) milk
1 oz (25 g) margarine or butter

Heat the oven to 350F (180C) gas 4. Thinly slice the potatoes and onion. Layer them in a greased, ovenproof dish, seasoning as you go. Pour in the milk to reach just below the top layer of potatoes. Dot the top with margarine or butter and put the dish into the oven for 1½ hours or until the potatoes are tender.

Braised celery

¾ head celery
Salt and pepper
¼ pint (150 ml) stock
½ oz (15 g) margarine

Heat the oven to 350F (180C) gas 4. Cut the celery sticks into short lengths and put them into an ovenproof dish. Season, pour in the stock and dot with the margarine. Cover the dish and put it into the oven for 1½ hours, or until the celery is tender.

Broccoli

1 lb (450 g) broccoli
½ oz (15 g) butter or margarine

Divide the broccoli into small fleurettes. Boil until tender, about 15 minutes. Drain and serve with a knob of butter or margarine.

Spring cabbage

1 lb (450 g) spring cabbage
Freshly-ground black pepper
½ oz (15 g) butter or margarine

Cut the cabbage into sections and boil them until they are just tender, about 15 minutes. Chop, and add a sprinkling of black pepper and a knob of butter or margarine.

Caramelised apples

1½ lb (675 g) cooking apples
6 tablespoons (90 ml) water
¼ pint (150 ml) whipping cream, whipped
6 oz (175 g) soft brown sugar

Peel, core and chop the apples. Put them into a saucepan with the water, cover them and set them on a low heat for 15 minutes or until they are soft. Rub them through a sieve. There should be about 12 oz (350 g). Cool them.

Divide the sieved apple between four ramekin dishes. Cover them first with a thick layer of whipped cream and then a thick layer of soft brown sugar. Chill overnight in the refrigerator.

For serving, preheat the grill to high. Place the ramekins under the grill until the sugar melts and caramelises.

This dessert can be eaten cold but the hot and cold effect, if it is eaten straight away, is unusual and enjoyable.

Alternative: This recipe is also delicious using sliced fresh peaches.

Third prize winner
Isabel Clarke, York.

Curried lentil soup

Ham and curd envelopes
Cucumber and mushroom salad
Half loaf home-made sourdough bread
with butter

Mulled syllabub

To drink, beer, cider or apple juice with the money remaining
from the five pounds
Cost without drink, spring 1982: £3.40½

Contributor's note: Buy a small fore-shoulder joint of ham, of
which only about one third will be needed for the meal. The bet-
ter part can be used for sandwiches. Soak the ham overnight,
drain it and boil it in fresh water until tender. Lift out the ham
and reserve the stock. Cut away any fat from the ham. Finely
chop it and put it into a frying pan. Set it on a low heat to render
down to make fat for frying.

Curried lentil soup

4 oz (125 g) red lentils
One 8 oz (225 g) tin tomatoes
1 medium onion, finely chopped
1 teaspoon (5 ml) curry powder
½ pint (275 ml) ham stock
1 garlic clove, crushed
½ oz (15 g) butter
1 teaspoon (5 ml) paprika
¼ teaspoon (1.5 ml) mustard powder

Soak the lentils in cold water for 1 hour. Drain them. Put them into a saucepan with the tomatoes, onion, curry powder and stock. Bring them to the boil and cook them gently, covered, for 20 minutes. Add the garlic, butter, paprika and mustard powder and continue cooking for a further 10 minutes or until the lentils are soft.

Ham and curd envelopes

pancakes

1½ oz (40 g) dried milk powder
¾ pint (425 ml) water
6 oz (175 g) plain flour
Pinch salt
2 eggs
Ham fat for frying

filling

12 oz (350 g) curd cheese
2 eggs, beaten
6 oz (175 g) ham
2 tablespoons (30 ml) chopped parsley
2 tablespoons (30 ml) chopped chives
Salt and pepper

To make the pancakes, mix the milk powder with the water. Sift the flour and salt into a bowl and make a well in the centre. Beat in the eggs and then gradually beat in the milk until you have a smooth batter. Leave it to stand in a cool place for 30 minutes.

For the filling, put the curd cheese into a bowl and gradually beat in the eggs so the mixture is smooth. Mix in the ham and herbs and season.

Make 12–14 pancakes with the batter mixture, frying them in ham fat on one side only and turning them on to a plate so they are cooked side up, raw side down.

Put 1 tablespoon (15 ml) of the filling in the centre of each pancake. Fold the pancakes into an envelope shape. Fill the remaining pancakes in the same way. They can now be cooked straight away or stored in the refrigerator until needed, placed between sheets of polythene to prevent them sticking and covered with a further layer of polythene.

Fry the pancakes in ham fat or oil on a medium heat for 10–15 minutes, so they are golden brown on both sides. Serve them straight away.

Cucumber and mushroom salad

⅔ cucumber
4 oz (125 g) button mushrooms
¼ pint (150 ml) home-made yoghurt
1 tablespoon (15 ml) chopped dill
2 tablespoons (30 ml) chopped chives
1 teaspoon (15 ml) sugar
Salt and pepper

Finely slice the cucumber and mushrooms. To make the dressing, beat together the yoghurt, herbs, sugar and seasonings. Fold the dressing into the salad just before serving.

Editor's note: Bought yoghurt may be used instead of home-made.

Mulled syllabub

½ pint (275 ml) home-made elderberry wine
4 cloves
3 inch (7.5 cm) cinnamon stick
Thinly pared rind 1 lemon
1 dessertspoon (10 ml) honey
1 oz (25 g) cornflour
5 tablespoons (75 ml) double cream
Tops from 2 bottles milk
1 egg yolk
2 egg whites
4 muscatel raisins soaked in elderberry wine (optional)

Put the wine into a saucepan with the cloves, cinnamon, lemon rind and honey. Bring it to just below simmering point and hold it at that temperature for 10 minutes. Strain it and return it to the pan.

In a bowl, mix half the hot wine into the cornflour to make a smooth paste. Bring the rest of the wine to the boil. Add the cornflour mixture and stir on a low heat until you have a thick sauce. Take the pan from the heat and let the sauce cool.

Beat in the egg yolk. Stiffly beat the egg whites and fold them into the cold sauce. Beat the double cream until it is thick. Gradually beat in the tops of the milk. Fold two thirds of this cream mixture into the syllabub.

Serve the syllabub in sundae dishes with a spoonful of the remaining cream on top. Garnish, if liked, with the soaked raisins.

Editor's note: Any rich, red, home-made wine could be used for this. Otherwise, use a cheap but full-bodied bought red wine and double the amount of honey.

Honourable mention

Mrs Joan Holgate, Merstham, Surrey.

Watercress soup
Wholemeal rolls

❦

Gourmet beef casserole
Green salad or
runner beans or courgettes

❦

Lemon mint ice cream

❦

Coffee

Cost, spring 1982: £4.87½

Watercress soup

2 medium potatoes
1½ pints (850 ml) water
2 chicken stock cubes, crumbled
1 bunch watercress
4 wholemeal rolls for serving

Cut the potatoes into small pieces. Simmer them until tender in lightly-salted water taken from the 1½ pints (850 ml). Chop the watercress, reserving four small sprigs for garnish.

Put the potatoes, cooking water, remaining water, crumbled stock cubes and chopped watercress into a liquidiser and work them until you have a smooth soup.

Reheat, without boiling. Serve with wholemeal rolls.

Gourmet beef casserole

Contributor's note: These quantities will serve six people, so freeze the remainder to provide a meal for two at a later date. The casserole reheats well so can be prepared the day before. To feed vegetarians, substitute the equivalent amount of soya mince for the minced beef.

8 oz (225 g) tagliatelle
1 teaspoon (5 ml) vegetable oil
1 lb (450 g) best minced beef
One 1 lb (450 g) tin tomatoes
½ green pepper, chopped
4 medium mushrooms, chopped
3½ fl oz (100 ml) Burgundy (optional)
One 5 oz (150 g) tin tomato paste
1 garlic clove, finely chopped
2 teaspoons (10 ml) sugar
One 3 oz (75 g) packet Philadelphia cream cheese
7 fl oz (200 ml) soured cream
1 large onion, finely chopped
3 oz (75 g) Cheddar cheese, grated

Heat the oven to 350F (180C) gas 4. Cook the tagliatelle in lightly-salted water until tender – about 15 minutes. Drain it.

Heat the oil in a frying pan on a high heat. Put in the beef and break it up with a fork. Cook it, stirring frequently, until it loses its red colour. Stir in the tomatoes, pepper, mushrooms, wine, tomato paste, garlic and sugar. Simmer, uncovered, for 10 minutes.

Beat the cream cheese in a bowl to make it soft. Gradually beat in the soured cream. Stir in the onion and tagliatelle.

Pour about 7 fl oz (200 ml) of the meat sauce into a 6-pint (3.6 litre) casserole. Cover it with a layer of the tagliatelle mixture and then sprinkle on a layer of Cheddar cheese. Repeat the layers, ending with meat sauce and a sprinkling of Cheddar. Cover the casserole and put it into the oven for 40 minutes.

Accompaniments: This is a filling dish and needs little to accompany it. A crisp mixed salad goes well in summer, and in winter a crunchy salad made of chopped fennel, apple, celery, onion, walnuts and parsley in a vinaigrette dressing.

Runner beans go particularly well, as do very lightly-cooked courgettes.

Lemon mint ice cream

(This was a recipe originally broadcast on *Woman's Hour* in 1981.)
Contributor's note: This will serve eight, so reserve half for another day.

4 large eggs, separated
4 oz (125 g) caster sugar
½ pint (275 ml) double cream
grated rind and juice 2 lemons
3 tablespoons (45 ml) chopped mint

Lightly beat the egg yolks with a fork. Stiffly whip the egg whites. Add the caster sugar to the whites 1 tablespoon (15 ml) at a time, whisking after each addition. Whisk until the mixture is firm and stands up in peaks (about 5 minutes with an electric beater). Gently stir in the egg yolks.

Whisk together the cream, lemon rind and juice until the mixture is really foamy. Fold the egg mixture into the cream mixture, together with the mint.

Pour the mixture into a 2½-pint (1.5 litre) container and freeze it.

Allow the ice to thaw very slightly in the refrigerator before serving. If you take it out of the freezer just before serving the soup it will be just right.

Honourable mention

Mrs Caroline Stay, York.

*Mussels with caramelised apples
and yoghurt*
Home-made crusty bread

― ❦ ―

Fettuce soufflé
Green salad

― ❦ ―

Wild blackberry and almond shortcake

Cost, spring 1982: £4.18

Mussels with caramelised apples and yoghurt

3 lb (1.35 kg) live mussels
8 fl oz (225 ml) cider or water
1 large, firm eating apple
3 oz (75 g) Krona margarine
2 teaspoons (10 ml) sugar
Salt and pepper
juice ½ lemon
¼ pint (150 ml) natural yoghurt
2 tablespoons (30 ml) chopped chives

To prepare the mussels, scrub them and remove the beards. Put them into a saucepan with the cider or water and set them on a moderate heat until they open, about 7 minutes. Drain them and discard any that have not opened. Take the rest from the shells.

Core (don't peel) and thinly slice the apple. Melt half the margarine in a frying pan on a medium heat. Toss the apple rings in it until they are golden and just soft, don't overcook. Add the sugar and allow it to caramelise. Take the pan from the heat.

Melt the remaining margarine in a saucepan and toss the mussels in it until they are well heated through. Add the apple rings, seasoning and lemon juice. Take the pan from the heat.

Divide the mussels between four individual bowls. Sprinkle them with chives. Serve with home-made, crusty bread and a bowl of chilled yoghurt.

Fettuce soufflé

1 smoked ham shank
1 lb (450 g) spinach
4 oz (125 g) fettuce
1½ lb (675 g) tomatoes
1 garlic clove, crushed
1 teaspoon (5 ml) dried basil
Salt and pepper
¼ pint (150 ml) soured cream
1½ oz (40 g) Krona margarine

1½ oz (40 g) flour
7 fl oz (200 ml) milk
1 teaspoon (5 ml) granular mustard
1 bayleaf
1 oz (25 g) Parmesan cheese, grated
3 large eggs, separated

Put the ham shank into a saucepan and cover it with water. Bring it to the boil and simmer it for 1–1½ hours or until tender. Remove it and reserve the stock for soup. Cut the meat into small dice, discarding all the fat and gristle.

Heat the oven to 375F (190C) gas 5. Trim the spinach and put it into boiling water for 1 minute. Drain it. Cook the fettuce in lightly-salted boiling water until just tender, about 15 minutes. Drain it. Scald, skin and slice the tomatoes.

Line a large, greased soufflé dish with the spinach. Put in half the tomatoes, all the pasta and ham and then the remaining tomatoes. Season, as you make the layers, with the garlic, basil and salt and pepper. Spread the soured cream on top.

For the soufflé mixture, melt the margarine in a saucepan on a medium heat. Stir in the flour and milk. Bring to the boil, stirring, and stir until you have a thick sauce. Add the mustard and bayleaf and season. Simmer very gently, stirring frequently, for 10 minutes.

Take the pan from the heat and remove the bayleaf. Beat in three quarters of the Parmesan cheese. Beat in the egg yolks, one at a time. Stiffly whip the egg whites and fold them into the mixture.

Spoon the soufflé mixture over the pasta and tomato layers and sprinkle the top with the remaining Parmesan cheese. Bake the soufflé for 45 minutes, or until it is risen and golden brown.

Editor's note: Fettuce is a ribbon-shaped pasta. Tagliatelle is a good substitute, if fettuce is unavailable.

Wild blackberry and almond shortcake

1 lb (450 g) blackberries
3½ oz (100 g) caster sugar
3 oz (75 g) Krona margarine
4½ oz (130 g) plain flour
Pinch salt
2 oz (50 g) blanched almonds
Whipped cream (optional)

Heat the oven to 375F (190C) gas 5. Wash the blackberries and drain them well. Toss them with 2 oz (50 g) of the caster sugar and chill them.

To make the shortcake, soften the margarine and beat in the sugar. Work in the sifted flour and salt so the mixture becomes a paste. Press the paste into the base and sides of a greased 7-inch (18 cm) flan dish. Neaten the top edge and prick the base all over with a fork. Bake for 30–35 minutes or until firm and pale golden.

While the base is cooking, halve the almonds and toast them under a high grill, watching carefully so that they do not burn. Cool them.

Take the shortcake from the oven. Pile on the blackberries and sprinkle them with the almonds. Serve immediately, with whipped cream.

Contributor's note: The shortcake must be served very hot and the blackberries very cold, for half the delight is in the contrast.

Soups and starters

Cold avocado soup

2 ripe avocados, peeled and stoned
¾ pint (425 ml) vegetable stock
7 fl oz (200 ml) milk
7 fl oz (200 ml) natural yoghurt
1 tablespoon (15 ml) lemon juice
Pinch garlic salt
¼ teaspoon (1.5 ml) chilli powder
2 tablespoons (30 ml) chopped fresh chives

Put all the ingredients, except the chives, into a blender or food processor. Buzz until smooth. Chill. Serve in individual bowls, garnished with chopped chives.

Mrs Syrel Dawson, London SW19.

Chilled cucumber and grapefruit soup

2 large cucumbers
2 grapefruit
½ pint (275 ml) natural yoghurt
Salt and pepper
Ice cubes
2 tablespoons chopped mint

Grate the cucumbers without skinning them or losing their liquid but discarding the large seeds. Season and leave for 2 hours. Cut away the peel and pith from the grapefruit. Cut the segments away from the skin and pick out the pips.

Put the grapefruit into a blender. Add the cucumber and yoghurt and blend well. Serve the soup with ice cubes floating in it and sprinkled with fresh mint.

This is a sharp and lively soup; very refreshing.

Mrs E. M. Monckton, Wrington, Avon.

Broccoli and watercress soup

8 oz (225 g) sprouting broccoli
1 bunch watercress
One 8 oz (225 g) potato
1 oz (25 g) butter
1 medium onion, finely chopped
1 pint (575 ml) chicken stock, hot
Up to ½ pint (275 ml) milk
Salt and freshly-ground black pepper

Wash and trim the heads of broccoli, cutting away the main part of the hard stem. Wash the watercress, cutting away the bottom of the stalks. Chop the watercress, keeping aside a little for garnish. Peel and dice the potato.

Melt the butter in a saucepan on a low heat. Add the onion, cover and cook gently for 5 minutes, or until soft. Add the watercress, broccoli and potato and toss them around for ½ minute. Pour in the hot stock, bring to the boil, cover and simmer gently for 30 minutes.

Pass the soup through a vegetable mill. Return it to the saucepan, stir in milk to taste and season. Reheat without boiling.

Serve in individual bowls, garnished with the reserved watercress. This soup looks best in small soup coupes, or white lotus bowls.

Mrs E. R. I. Hanning, Newbury, Berks.

Fish soup

12 oz (350 g) white fish fillets (suggest cheap fish such as whiting or coley)
Juice 1 lemon
Salt and pepper
2 pints (1.15 litres) water or stock
2 tablespoons (30 ml) oil
2 celery sticks plus leaves, chopped
3 carrots, chopped
1 large onion, chopped
1 egg

Cut the fish into 1–1½ inch (2.5–4 cm) pieces. Rub them with a little of the lemon juice and season. Bring the water or stock to the boil in a saucepan. Add the oil and vegetables and simmer for 30 minutes. Add the fish and cook for a further 20 minutes. Strain the soup. Reserve the vegetables and fish and keep them warm. Return the liquid to the saucepan.

Beat the egg and slowly beat in 2 tablespoons (30 ml) lemon juice. Stir in 2 tablespoons (30 ml) of the hot liquid and pour the mixture into the saucepan. Stir on a low heat, without boiling, for 2 minutes.

Put the fish and vegetables into four soup dishes and pour the soup over the top.

Jenny Buels, Llanllechid, Gwynedd.

Spicy chicken and vegetable soup

2 sets chicken giblets
1½ pints (850 ml) chicken stock (preferably home-made as the result of poaching a chicken as in *Avocado Creamed Chicken* page 60; alternatively made from 1½ pints (850 ml) water and 1 chicken stock cube)
Salt and pepper
Pinch ground mace
2 tablespoons (30 ml) chopped chervil (optional)
2 tablespoons (30 ml) tomato purée
1 medium onion, finely chopped
4 celery sticks, finely chopped
1 teaspoon (5 ml) curry powder
1 medium carrot, shredded
1 medium parsnip, shredded
4 tablespoons (60 ml) chopped parsley

Clean and chop the giblets, except for the necks which should be put in whole. Put them into a saucepan with the stock. Bring them to the boil. Remove any scum that rises to surface. Season, and add the mace, chervil, tomato purée, onion and celery. Simmer for 1 hour.

Lift out the neck pieces. Take the meat from the bones, chop it and return it to the saucepan. Add the curry powder, carrot and parsnip and cook for a further 20 minutes. Serve scattered with chopped parsley.

Contributor's note: The flavour will improve if the soup can be refrigerated overnight and gently heated just before serving.

Editor's note: Parsley may be used instead of chervil in the recipe.

Maralyn Heathcock, Hagley, West Midlands.

Pork and lentil soup

2 pints (1.15 litres) pork stock
Liquid drained from one 14 oz (400 g) tin tomatoes
Salt and pepper
4 oz (125 g) split red lentils
1 large onion, thinly sliced

Put the stock and tomato liquid into a pressure cooker or saucepan and bring them to the boil. Add the onion and lentils. Stir well, season and cover. Cook for 30 minutes in a pressure cooker or 1 hour in a saucepan.

Contributor's note: The stock is made from the bones and trimmings of the pig's head used for *Orangey pork casserole* (page 63). Using a pressure cooker or large pan with a well-fitting lid, cook all the bones and trimmings with 2½ pints (1.425 litres) water, seasoning, half an onion and sprigs of herbs such as thyme, rosemary and sage. Cook for 40 minutes in a pressure cooker or 1½ hours in a saucepan. Drain carefully.

Mrs Jill Kemp, Chester.

Beef and onion soup

| 2 oz (50 g) beef drink concentrate |
| 2 tablespoons (30 ml) tomato purée |
| 2¼ pints (1.3 litres) hot water |
| 14 oz (400 g) onions, finely chopped |
| 1–2 garlic cloves, finely chopped |
| Salt and pepper |
| 4 tablespoons (60 ml) chopped parsley |

In a saucepan, stir the concentrate and the tomato purée into the hot water, add the chopped onions and garlic, and season. Bring them to the boil and simmer gently, partially covered, for 35 minutes. The soup can then be left as it is or blended if required.
  Serve the soup hot, sprinkled generously with parsley.

Contributor's note: It is a good idea to make the soup the night before to allow the flavours to blend. It is a tasty, nourishing soup and good for slimmers.

Louise Clark, Glasgow.

Baked grapefruit starter

2 grapefruit
4 oz (125 g) smoked bacon pieces
4 oz (125 g) cooked spinach, chopped
1 tablespoon (15 ml) natural yoghurt
1 teaspoon (5 ml) Worcestershire sauce
¼ teaspoon (1.5 ml) ground nutmeg
Salt and pepper

Heat the oven to 350F (180C) gas 4. Cut each grapefruit in half. Take out the flesh, cut it from the skin and chop it. Put it into a bowl. Gently fry the bacon until cooked through but not brown. Cool, and finely chop it.

   Mix the grapefruit with the spinach, yoghurt, Worcestershire sauce, nutmeg and seasonings. Pile the mixture into the grapefruit shells and sprinkle the bacon on top. Put the stuffed shells on to a heatproof dish and put them into the oven for 25 minutes.

Editor's note: 4 oz (125 g) frozen spinach may be used for this recipe; or cook 8 oz (225 g) fresh spinach leaves.

Mrs B. Ferguson, Bridgwater, Somerset.

Cottage strawberry avocados

2 ripe avocados
Juice ½ lemon
8 oz (225 g) strawberries, fresh or frozen
5 oz (150 g) cottage cheese
Salt and pepper
2 teaspoons (10 ml) finely-chopped mint
4 mint leaves

Halve and stone the avocados. Scoop out and mash the flesh. Paint the inside of the shells with lemon juice to prevent them from discolouring. Reserve four strawberries for garnish.

Mix together the mashed avocado, the strawberries and the cottage cheese. Mash with a fork and season. Pile the mixture into the avocado shells and sprinkle it with the chopped mint. Garnish each filled shell with a mint leaf and a whole strawberry.

Muriel A. Constable, Blacon, Chester.

Butterbean and mushroom salad with garlic bread

4 oz (125 g) butterbeans
4 oz (125 g) button mushrooms
3 tablespoons (45 ml) oil
1 tablespoon (15 ml) white wine vinegar
½ teaspoon (2.5 ml) French mustard
½ garlic clove, crushed
Salt and pepper
½ oz (15 g) parsley, finely chopped
1 teaspoon (5 ml) ground coriander
garlic bread
½ French loaf
4 oz (125 g) butter, softened
2 garlic cloves, crushed

Soak the butterbeans for a few hours. Drain and rinse them and cook until soft but not mushy. Drain. Wipe the mushrooms and cut them in half. Mix them with the beans.

Beat together the oil, vinegar, garlic and seasonings. Pour them over the beans and mushrooms. Mix in the parsley and coriander and leave the salad until the beans are cold.

For the loaf, heat the oven to 425F (220C) gas 7. Slit the loaf down the middle and open it out. Beat the garlic into the butter and spread the mixture over the loaf. Reshape the loaf and wrap it in aluminium foil. Bake it for 15 minutes. Cut it into four sections and serve hot with the salad.

Janet Daly, Cardiff.

Salad jelly

1 lemon jelly
1 small grapefruit
½ cucumber
2 medium carrots, cooked until just tender
1 tablespoon (15 ml) cooked peas
1 lettuce, shredded
4 tablespoons (60 ml) mayonnaise

Melt the jelly and cool it. Cut the rind and pith from the grapefruit. Cut the segments away from the skin. Dice the cucumber and carrots.

When the jelly is on the point of setting, fold in the grapefruit, cucumber, carrots and peas. Pour the mixture into four oiled individual moulds or cups and leave them in a cool place for 1 hour for the jelly to set.

Arrange a bed of shredded lettuce on each of four small plates. Turn the jellies on to the lettuce and decorate them with the mayonnaise.

Mrs Margaret M. Pattison. London E11.

Smoked haddock envelopes

8 oz (225 g) smoked haddock fillet
½ pint (275 ml) milk
1 oz (25 g) flour
1 oz (25 g) margarine
One 7½ oz (215 g) packet frozen puff pastry, defrosted

Put the fish into a saucepan with the milk. Bring it gently to the boil and simmer it for 2 minutes. Take the pan from the heat and leave the fish in the milk for 30 minutes. Lift it out, skin, bone and flake it. Strain and reserve the milk.

Melt the margarine in a saucepan. Take it from the heat and stir in the flour. Gradually stir in the milk. Return the pan to the heat and stir until the sauce thickens. Take it from the heat again and stir in the fish.

Roll out the pastry thinly to make a 13-inch (32 cm) square. Cut it into four small squares. Put a portion of the fish mixture into the centre of each square. Wet the edges of the pastry. Fold the corners to the centre and pinch the edges firmly together to make a square envelope. Refrigerate until needed.

Heat the oven to 350F (180C) gas 4. Place the fish envelopes on a dampened baking sheet and bake them for 20–25 minutes or until golden brown.

Mrs J. E. Porter, Reading, Berks.

Devilled fish with shrimp sauce

1 lb (450 g) coley fillet
¼ pint dry white wine or white wine vinegar
1 tablespoon (15 ml) tomato purée
1 shallot, finely chopped
½ teaspoon (2.5 ml) made mustard
½ teaspoon (2.5 ml) soft brown sugar
1 tablespoon (15 ml) mango chutney
½ oz (15 g) butter
½ oz (15 g) flour
Up to ½ pint (275 ml) top of the milk
3 oz (75 g) peeled shrimps

Heat the oven to 350F (180C) gas 4. Cut the coley into four equal-sized pieces and put them into an ovenproof dish. Mix together the wine (or vinegar), tomato purée, shallot, mustard, sugar and mango chutney. Spoon the mixture over the fish. Cover with foil or a lid and bake for 20 minutes. Lift the fish on to a serving plate and keep it warm.

Measure the liquid from the baking dish and make it up to ½ pint (275 ml) with top of the milk. Melt the butter in a saucepan on a medium heat. Stir in the flour and then the milk mixture. Bring them to the boil, stirring. Simmer for 2 minutes, stirring frequently. Add the shrimps and pour the sauce over the coley.

Mrs Margaret Davies, London NW8.

Mackerel with yoghurt and garlic

1 mackerel, weighing about 1 lb (450 g)
Salt and freshly-ground black pepper
Margarine for greasing
¼ pint (150 ml) natural yoghurt
2 garlic cloves, crushed
4 slices cucumber

Heat the oven to 350F (180C) gas 4. Heat the grill to high. Remove the head and tail from the mackerel. Slit the fish open, place it on a board, skin side up, and press along the centre back. Remove the back bone, fins and any other large bones. Cut the mackerel into two fillets and cut each one in half crossways. Season.

Grease a shallow, ovenproof dish with margarine. Put in the fillets, skin side down. Grill them until the flesh turns white, about 2 minutes.

Mix the yoghurt with the garlic and season. Spread the mixture over the mackerel. Cover and cook on the bottom shelf of the oven for 30 minutes.

Make the cucumber into twists and use them to garnish the mackerel.

Mrs Jill Kemp, Chester.

Fish salad

12 oz (350 g) coley fillets
4 small tomatoes
8 oz (225 g) runner beans, fresh or frozen
2 tablespoons (30 ml) oil
1 tablespoon (15 ml) white wine vinegar
Salt and pepper
1 very small onion, grated
¼ pint (150 ml) natural yoghurt
4 thin slices brown bread, buttered

Put the coley into a saucepan and cover it with water. Bring it gently to the boil and simmer it for 5 minutes or until cooked through. Lift it out, skin and bone it, flake it and cool it.

Scald, skin and quarter the tomatoes. Cook the beans until they are just tender. Beat together the oil and vinegar. Season them and fold them into the beans and tomatoes. Arrange the salad round the edge of a serving dish.

Mix the coley with the onion and yoghurt and pile it into the centre of the dish. Chill for 1 hour. Serve with brown bread and butter.

Jill Adams, Winchester, Hants.

Smoked mackerel pâté

| 8 oz (225 g) smoked mackerel fillet |
| 3 oz (75 g) margarine |
| Juice ½ lemon |
| Salt and freshly-ground black pepper |

Bone and mash the mackerel. Gently melt the margarine. Beat it into the mackerel. Mix in the lemon juice and season to taste.

Press the pâté into a dish and chill it in the refrigerator for about 1 hour or until firm.

Editor's note: If a soft margarine is used there is no need to melt it.

Janet Skea, London SW1.

Salmon pâté

| One 7 oz (200 g) tin pink salmon |
| 1 egg, hard-boiled |
| 2 teaspoons (10 ml) tomato purée |
| 1 teaspoon (5 ml) chopped fresh basil or pinch dried |
| Salt and freshly-ground black pepper |

Drain off and reserve the liquid from the salmon. Mash both the salmon and the hard-boiled egg and mix them together. Beat in the tomato purée, basil and seasonings and enough of the reserved liquid to make a smooth pâté. It should not be too dry.

Press the pâté into a dish and chill it in the refrigerator for about 1 hour or until firm.

Janet Skea, London SW1.

Pilchard mousse

One 7 oz (200 g) tin pilchards in tomato sauce
½ oz (15 g) gelatin
2 tablespoons (30 ml) stock
¾ oz (20 g) butter
1 small onion, quartered
¾ oz (20 g) flour
½ pint (575 ml) milk
1 bayleaf
Salt and pepper
2 tablespoons (30 ml) mayonnaise
1 egg white, stiffly whipped
4 thin slices cucumber
4 slices bread, buttered and cut into triangles

Drain the pilchards. Bone and flake them. In a small pan, soak the gelatin in the stock.

Melt the butter in a saucepan on a low heat. Put in the pieces of onion and cook them for 1 minute. Stir in the flour and milk and add the bayleaf. Bring the sauce to the boil, stirring. Season and simmer for 2 minutes. Take the pan from the heat. Cool the sauce and discard the onion and bayleaf.

In a bowl, mix the mayonnaise into the flaked fish. Season and mix in the sauce. Gently melt the gelatin and stir it into the mixture. Fold in the egg white.

Pour the mixture into four small ramekin dishes and leave it in a cool place for about 2 hours to set. Garnish each mousse with a thin slice of cucumber, made into a twist. Serve the bread separately.

Mrs M. Sponar, Heacham, Norfolk.

Tuna and fennel mousse

1 tablespoon (15 ml) gelatin
2 tablespoons (30 ml) vinegar
½ pint (275 ml) boiling water
1 chicken stock cube
One 7 oz (200 g) tin tuna fish, drained and mashed
1 small onion, finely chopped
½ teaspoon (2.5 ml) garlic salt
½ teaspoon (2.5 ml) ground fennel
Pepper
5 tablespoons (75 ml) natural yoghurt

garnish
¼ cucumber, thinly sliced
4 tomatoes, thinly sliced
2 tablespoons (30 ml) chopped chives

In a large bowl, dissolve the gelatin in the vinegar. Add the boiling water and stock cube and whisk until the gelatin has melted. Add the tuna, onion, garlic salt and fennel and season with pepper. Whisk for 1 minute. Leave the mixture in a cool place until it is cold and beginning to set. Fold in the yoghurt.

Turn the mousse into four individual ramekin (or similar) dishes and cover with cling film. Put the mousses in the refrigerator for about 1 hour to set.

Turn them out on to individual plates. Arrange cucumber and tomato slices around the edge and sprinkle the chives over the top.

Mrs J. L. Bacon, Westone, Northampton.

Chicken liver mousse with tomato sauce

6 oz (175 g) chicken livers
1 oz (25 g) skimmed milk powder
¼ pint (150 ml) chicken stock
½ medium onion, finely chopped
1 garlic clove, finely chopped
Pinch ground nutmeg
1 tablespoon (15 ml) chopped parsley
Salt and pepper
4 black olives

Tomato sauce
Half 13 oz (375 g) tin tomatoes
½ medium onion, finely chopped
1 garlic clove, finely chopped
1 teaspoon (5 ml) oil
¼ teaspoon (1.5 ml) sugar
Pinch dried oregano
¼ pint (150 ml) chicken stock
Juice ½ medium orange

Heat the oven to 425F (220C) gas 7. Trim and chop the chicken livers. Dissolve the skimmed milk in the stock. Put the livers, stock mixture, onion, garlic, nutmeg and half the parsley into a blender or food processor. Season and blend until smooth.

Pour the mixture into four greased ramekin dishes. Cover each one with foil and stand them in a baking tin of water. Bake for 30 minutes or until set.

Turn each mousse on to a hot plate. Pour a little sauce over each one. Scatter them with the remaining parsley and top with an olive.

To make the tomato sauce
In a saucepan, soften the onion and garlic in the oil. Add the tomatoes and all the remaining ingredients. Simmer the sauce for 10–15 minutes so it is thickened and reduced by about half.

Patsy Nightingale, London N4.

Surprise soufflé patties
with épinards à la grecque

Surprise soufflé patties

2½ oz (65 g) butter, at room temperature, plus extra for greasing
2 eggs, separated
3 oz (75 g) flour
2 oz (50 g) Cheddar cheese, grated
Salt and pepper
½ oz (15 g) fresh yeast
4 tablespoons (60 ml) single cream
1 oz (25 g) ham
2 oz (50 g) sausagemeat
2 teaspoons (10 ml) chopped fresh parsley, or 1 teaspoon (5 ml) dried

Epinards à la grecque

1 lb (450 g) spinach
1 tablespoon (15 ml) olive oil
1 tablespoon (15 ml) lemon juice
Salt and pepper
Freshly-grated nutmeg

For the patties, heat the oven to 350F (180C) gas 4. Beat 2 oz (50 g) of the butter until soft. Beat in one egg yolk then half the flour. Beat until smooth, then add the other egg yolk and remainder of the flour. Beat in the grated cheese and season. Dissolve the yeast in the cream and stir into the mixture. Stiffly whip the egg whites and fold them in carefully.

Finely chop the ham and mix it with the sausagemeat, parsley and remaining butter. Grease four patty tins or ramekin dishes. Spoon half the soufflé mixture into them. Divide all the ham mixture between them and top with the remaining soufflé mixture. Bake the patties for 30 minutes. Cool them for 5 minutes and turn them out (see below).

For the Epinards à la grecque, wash and chop the spinach. Heat the oil in a saucepan on a low heat. Stir in the spinach, cover and cook for 5 minutes, stirring occasionally. Add the lemon juice and season.

To serve, place the spinach in the centre of a large serving dish and grate a little nutmeg over the top. Arrange the patties around the spinach.

Diana Jones, London N3.

Main dishes

Morue à l'Irlandaise

1½ lb (675 g) cod (or other white fish such as coley or haddock)
1½ lb (675 g) potatoes
1 egg, lightly beaten
¼ pint (150 ml) milk
1½ oz (40 g) butter
8 oz (225 g) onions
1½ oz (40 g) flour
4 tablespoons (60 ml) single cream
1 tablespoon (15 ml) chopped chives (or more to taste)
2 tablespoons (30 ml) chopped parsley
Salt and pepper
½ pint (275 ml) Guinness (or other stout)
½ red pepper

Heat the oven to 350F (180C) gas 4. Cut the fish into 2-inch (5 cm) pieces. Peel the potatoes and boil them until tender. Mash them with the egg and milk.

Melt the butter in a saucepan on a low heat. Put in the onion and soften it. Stir in the flour and cook it for 2 minutes. Add the cream, fish and herbs and season. Take the pan from the heat and, after 5 minutes, stir in the Guinness.

Put the mixture into a greased casserole dish. Cover it completely with the mashed potato and make patterns on the top with a fork. Cut the red pepper into strips and arrange them in a flower shape on top of the potatoes. Bake for 30 minutes, or until the top has browned slightly.

Contributor's note: This constitutes a complete course in itself.

Diana Jones, London N3.

Stuffed fish casserole

1½ lb (675 g) white fish, in four equal-sized fillets

stuffing
3 oz (75 g) fresh brown or white bread crumbs
2 egg yolks
1 oz (25 g) chopped parsley (or a mixture of parsley and fennel leaves)
Salt and pepper

sauce
1 medium onion, finely chopped
2 oz (50 g) butter or bacon fat
8 oz (225 g) mushrooms, thinly sliced
One 14 oz (400 g) tin tomatoes
3 tablespoons (45 ml) natural yoghurt
Salt and pepper

Heat the oven to 350F (180C) gas 4. Skin the fish. Mix all the stuffing ingredients together. Divide the stuffing into four portions. Fold each fish fillet round a portion of stuffing.

For the sauce, gently cook the onion in the butter until transparent, about 2 minutes. Add the mushrooms and cook for a further 2 minutes, or until they shrink slightly. Pour in the tomatoes, together with their liquid. Mix in the yoghurt and season.

Pour the sauce into a casserole and arrange the stuffed fish fillets on top. Cover the casserole and put it into the oven for 30 minutes.

Serve with either jacket potatoes or plainly boiled brown or white rice.

Contributor's note: The type of fish used is a matter of taste. Whiting, coley or sole could be used. I can buy Torbay sole for 86p a pound.

Editor's note: If the parcels of fish look as though they might unfold during cooking, secure them with cocktail sticks.

Mrs B. Ferguson, Bridgwater, Somerset.

Fish mollie with rice

1 lb (450 g) coley fillet
1 tablespoon (15 ml) oil
2 medium onions, finely chopped
1 garlic clove, finely chopped
1 teaspoon (5 ml) ground ginger
1 teaspoon (5 ml) ground turmeric
1 teaspoon (5 ml) chilli powder
1 teaspoon (5 ml) ground cumin
1 teaspoon (5 ml) salt
1 teaspoon (5 ml) demerara sugar
½ packet dried mushroom soup
Half 13 oz (325 g) tin tomatoes
½ pint (275 ml) milk
4 oz (125 g) creamed coconut
6 tablespoons (90 ml) boiling water
10 oz (300 g) brown rice, boiled until tender and drained

Skin and bone the fish and cut it into ¾ inch (2 cm) cubes. Heat the oil in a large saucepan on a low heat. Put in the onions and garlic and fry them gently for 10 minutes. Stir in the spices, salt, sugar, soup powder, milk and tomatoes. Simmer, uncovered, stirring frequently, for 20 minutes. Add a little water if the sauce becomes too thick.

Fold in the fish and cook for a futher 10 minutes. Dissolve the creamed coconut in the boiling water. Stir it into the mixture and cook for 1 minute more.

Arrange a bed of cooked rice on a warmed serving dish and spoon the Fish mollie on top. Serve with *Lettuce and caper salad* (page 81).

Editor's note: Creamed coconut is sold in 7 oz (200 g) blocks, looking rather like white cooking fat. It can be bought in some major supermarkets besides delicatessens, health shops and Asian shops.

Patsy Nightingale, London N4.

Smoked haddock with brown rice

1½ lb (675 g) smoked haddock (or smoked cod)
10 oz (300 g) brown rice
8 oz (225 g) tomatoes
2 medium onions, roughly chopped
2 oz (50 g) butter
¼ pint (150 ml) soured cream
2 tablespoons (30 ml) chopped parsley or chives

Put the fish into a saucepan and cover it with cold water. Bring it gently to the boil and remove it from the heat. Leave it to stand for 10 minutes. Lift out the fish and reserve the liquid. Skin, bone and flake the fish.

Make the liquid up to 1¾ pints (725 ml) with cold water. Put it into a saucepan with the rice. Bring them to the boil. Season lightly. Cover and cook very gently for 45 minutes or until the rice is tender and all the liquid absorbed.

Finish the main dish while the rice is cooking. Scald, skin and chop the tomatoes. In a sauté pan or large frying pan, gently fry the onions in the butter until they are golden brown. Add the tomatoes and cook slowly for 4–5 minutes or until soft. Stir in the soured cream and the flaked fish. Heat through without boiling.

Make a circle of the cooked rice round the edge of a warmed serving dish. Spoon the fish mixture into the centre. Sprinkle the parsley or chives over the top.

Serve with *Glazed onions* (page 79).

Mrs E. R. I. Hanning, Newbury, Berks.

Smoked haddock roulade

8 oz (225 g) smoked haddock
½ pint (275 ml) milk
4 eggs, separated
4 tablespoons (60 ml) double cream
3 tablespoons (45 ml) grated Parmesan cheese

filling
1½ oz (40 g) butter
1 oz (25 g) flour
Milk from poaching fish
3 eggs, hard-boiled
1 tablespoon (15 ml) chopped parsley

Heat the oven to 400F (200C) gas 6. Line a 12 × 9-inch (30 × 23 cm) Swiss roll tin with buttered greaseproof paper. Put the smoked haddock into a saucepan. Pour in the milk and bring it to the boil. Simmer the haddock in the milk for 5 minutes. Lift it out and reserve the milk.

Skin and bone the haddock. Put it into a mixing bowl and mash it to a purée. Beat in the egg yolks, cream and 1 tablespoon (15 ml) of the cheese. Season to taste. Whip the three egg whites to stiff peaks and use a metal spoon to fold them gently into the fish mixture.

Turn the mixture into the prepared tin and spread it level. Sprinkle it with 1 tablespoon (15 ml) of the cheese and bake it for 10–15 minutes or until firm.

For the filling, melt the butter in a saucepan and stir in the flour. Stir for 1 minute and then stir in the milk. Beat well until the sauce comes to the boil. Simmer it gently for 2–3 minutes. Coarsely chop the hard-boiled eggs and add them to the sauce together with the parsley.

Lay a piece of greaseproof paper on a work surface and sprinkle it with the remaining cheese. Loosen the edges of the cooked roulade and turn it on to the paper. Peel away the lining paper and spread the surface of the roulade with the filling. Lift the underneath paper up at one narrow edge and roll up the roulade. Tilt it onto a hot serving dish and serve at once.

Serve with a tossed green salad and either new potatoes or *Baked potatoes with mint butter* page 80.

Contributor's note: The roulade mixture can be prepared an hour beforehand and popped into the oven as you sit down to the soup. The filling would be prepared at the same time and kept hot.

Mrs E. M. Monckton, Wrington, Avon.

Chicken and apricots

8 chicken pieces, thighs or drumsticks
One 12 oz (350 g) tin apricots
1 packet cream of leek soup powder

Heat the oven to 350F (180C) gas 4. Place the chicken pieces in a casserole. Drain the apricots and mix the syrup with the soup powder. Pour the mixture over the chicken and put the apricots on top. Cover the casserole and put it into the oven for 1 hour.

Serve with one 8 oz (225 g) packet egg noodles, cooked for 10 minutes in lightly-salted water and drained; together with lightly-boiled or steamed broccoli or courgettes.

Mrs Margaret M. Pattison, London E11.

Avocado creamed chicken

One 2½–3 lb (1.125–1.35 kg) chicken
1 garlic clove, cut
Salt and pepper
½ oz (15 g) butter
About 2½ pints (1.425 ml) water
1 small carrot, roughly chopped
1 small onion, roughly chopped
1 celery stick, roughly chopped

sauce
1 ripe avocado
1 garlic clove, crushed
½ pint (275 ml) low fat natural yoghurt
Juice ½ lemon
Salt and pepper
Dash Tabasco sauce
½ oz (15 g) flaked almonds, lightly toasted

Wash the chicken inside and out. Rub it with the cut clove of garlic and season it. Melt the butter in a heavy saucepan on a high heat. Put in the chicken and brown it all over. Pour in water to come approximately half-way up the chicken. Add the carrot, onion and celery stick. Cover tightly and simmer for 30 minutes. Turn the chicken over and simmer for a further 30 minutes or until the meat comes easily off the bone.

Lift out the chicken and reserve the stock for soup (see *Spicy chicken and vegetable soup* page 37). Whilst it is warm, take the meat off the bone and shred it. Arrange it on a serving dish.

For the sauce, chop the avocado and mix in with the garlic, yoghurt and lemon juice. Season lightly and add the Tabasco sauce. Liquidise to a smooth, pale green sauce. Pour the sauce over the chicken.

Warm the dish through in a preheated 325F (170C) gas 3 oven for 20 minutes. Just before serving, scatter it with the toasted almonds.

Serve with *Coleslaw* page 81.

Contributor's notes: The dish can also be served cold. When not counting costs, 2 tablespoons (30 ml) dry Martini can be added to the sauce.

Maralyn Heathcock, Hagley, West Midlands.

Assisi chicken with sweet and sour sauce

4 chicken joints
Juice and thinly-pared rind ½ lemon
Four 6-inch (10 cm) rosemary sprigs
Salt and pepper
½ oz (15 g) butter
Watercress for garnish

sauce
1 tablespoon (15 ml) oil
1 small onion, finely chopped
Half 14 oz (400 g) tin tomatoes
1 tablespoon (15 ml) tomato ketchup
1 tablespoon (15 ml) malt vinegar
1 tablespoon (15 ml) soft brown sugar
1 teaspoon (5 ml) made mustard
1 teaspoon (5 ml) Worcestershire sauce

Heat the oven to 400F (200C) gas 6. Place the chicken pieces, skin side down, in a shallow, ovenproof dish. Put in the lemon rind and pour in the juice. Place a rosemary sprig on each piece of chicken. Season and dot with butter. Cover the dish with foil or a lid and put it into the oven for 30 minutes. Turn the chicken pieces, cover again and cook for 15 minutes. Remove the cover and cook for a further 30 minutes.

Put the chicken pieces on to a hot plate. Strain the juices from the dish and skim them. Spoon them over the chicken. Garnish with watercress sprigs just before serving.

For the sauce
Heat the oil in a saucepan on a low heat. Put in the onion and cook it for 5 minutes. Add the remaining ingredients.

Bring them slowly to the boil and simmer them for 10 minutes, stirring occasionally. Serve the sauce hot, separately.

Serve with *Salad platter* (page 83) and 12 oz (350 g) patna rice, plainly boiled.

Mrs Vivienne Wayman, Stanmore, Middlesex.

Orangey pork casserole

½ pig's head, as lean as possible
1 orange
2 tablespoons (30 ml) vegetable oil
2 medium onions, thinly sliced
2 garlic cloves, finely chopped
1 dessert apple, peeled, cored and chopped
1 tablespoon (15 ml) soft brown sugar
2 tablespoons (30 ml) sultanas
4 fl oz (125 ml) strong cider
4 fl oz (125 ml) whey from yoghurt (see below)
4 fl oz (125 ml) vegetable stock
Salt and pepper

Have the bath chap taken from the pig's head. (Keep the bones and trimmings for *Pork and lentil soup* page 38). Singe the whiskers off with a flame or shave off with a sharp knife. Rinse well. Cut off the skin and the underlying fat. Season and set aside.

With a sharp knife, remove all the bones and gristle, taking care that no bone splinters are left. Rinse again and cut into small strips. Season well. Scrub the orange and grate the rind. Rub the rind into the pork pieces.

Heat the oven to 375F (190C) gas 5. Heat 1 tablespoon (15 ml) oil in a frying pan on a low heat. Put in the onions and garlic and cook them until they are lightly browned. Put them into a casserole. Add the remaining tablespoon (15 ml) oil to the frying pan and raise the heat. Put in the pork pieces and brown them on both sides. Put them into the casserole. Add the apple, sugar, sultanas and orange juice. Put the cider, whey and vegetable stock into the frying pan. Bring them to the boil, stirring in any residue in the pan. Pour them into the casserole. Taste and adjust the seasoning if necessary. Place the skin from the bath chap on top, fatty side down. Cover the casserole and put it into the oven for 1 hour 30 minutes, or until the meat is tender.

Keeping the casserole warm, remove the pork skin to a heat-proof dish, skin side up. Crisp it under a high grill taking care not to let it burn. With a sharp knife or scissors, cut it into small strips. Serve it in a separate dish.

Serve with either old potatoes baked in their jackets or new potatoes boiled with a mint sprig.

Whey from yoghurt: Bring 1½ pints (850 ml) milk to the boil and cool it to blood heat. Warm a wide-necked vacuum flask with hot water and dry it. Put in 1 tablespoon (15 ml) yoghurt and mix in a little of the milk. Add the remaining milk and mix well. Cover the flask and leave in a warm place for 8 hours. Empty the resulting yoghurt into a straining bag, suspend it over a bowl and leave it to drip overnight. The whey is the liquid that drips from the yoghurt. The thick yoghurt remaining in the bag can be used as a soft cheese as in *Lemon cheesecake* page 103.

Contributor's notes: The casserole can be effectively cooked in a slow cooker for 10 hours. If yoghurt whey is not available, extra vegetable stock may be used instead. Pork hocks may be used by the squeamish instead of a pig's head but they will be more expensive. Buy 1 litre Somerset strong cider. Use what you need for the recipe and serve the rest with the meal.

Mrs Jill Kemp, Chester.

Stuffed spare rib pork chops

4 pork spare rib chops or boneless pork steaks
1 oz (25 g) butter
1 medium onion, finely chopped
3 oz (75 g) fresh breadcrumbs (white or brown)
2 oz (50 g) mushrooms, finely chopped
2 oz (50 g) shelled walnuts, finely chopped
1 egg yolk
Salt and pepper
7 fl oz (200 ml) dry white wine or stock or a mixture of the two

Heat the oven to 375F (190C) gas 5. Holding one hand flat on top, slit each chop horizontally so it will open out like a book.

To make the stuffing, melt the butter in a frying pan on a low heat. Add the onion and mushrooms and cook them until the onion is soft. Take the pan from the heat and mix in the breadcrumbs, walnuts and egg yolk. Season. Lay the stuffing on one half of each chop. Close and reshape the chops. Tie them with strong thread or fine cotton string.

Put the chops into a baking dish and pour in the wine or stock. Cover and bake for 1 hour.

Serve with jacket potatoes, *Oven cooked carrots* page 79 and *Calabrese au gratin* page 78.

Contributor's note: Sage and onion stuffing may be used instead of mushroom.

Mrs Margaret Davies, London NW8.

Chinese spare ribs

2 lb (900 g) pork spare ribs
4 tablespoons (60 ml) oil
1 large onion, thinly sliced
½ green pepper, cut into 1 inch (2.5 cm) strips
Salt and pepper
2 tablespoons (30 ml) orange jelly marmalade
4 tablespoons (60 ml) soy sauce
1 garlic clove, crushed
½ pint (275 ml) chicken stock
1 tablespoon (15 ml) malt vinegar

for serving
One 8 oz (225 g) packet egg noodles
8 oz (225 g) frozen peas
3 large leeks
4 oz (125 g) button mushrooms
1 oz (25 g) butter

Heat the oven to 400F (200C) gas 6. Fry the spare ribs in the oil over a high heat until brown. Remove them and lower the heat. Gently soften the onion and pepper in the oil. Put them into a casserole and put the spare ribs on top. Season.

Mix together the marmalade, soy sauce and crushed garlic. Add the stock and vinegar and pour the mixture over the spare ribs. Cover the casserole and put it into the oven for 1 hour. Remove the lid and cook for a further 20 minutes.

Cook the noodles in lightly-salted boiling water for 10 minutes or until tender. Drain. Cook the frozen peas. Thinly slice the leeks and mushrooms and gently fry them in the butter until soft. Serve all these accompaniments separately.

Jill Adams, Winchester, Hants.

Baked liver with apricots and cheese

1½ lb (675 g) beef liver, in four slices
One 15 oz (425 g) tin apricot halves
1 teaspoon (5 ml) dried mixed herbs
1 teaspoon (5 ml) mustard powder
2 teaspoons (10 ml) soy sauce
1 tablespoon (15 ml) natural yoghurt
Grated rind ½ lemon
4 oz (125 g) fresh white breadcrumbs
Salt and pepper
2 oz (50 g) Cheddar cheese, grated
8 oz (225 g) Patna rice
2 tablespoons (30 ml) oil
1 medium onion, thinly sliced
8 oz (225 g) carrots, thinly sliced
8 oz (225 g) frozen peas
4 parsley sprigs

Soak the liver in cold water for 1 hour. Drain it and dry it with kitchen paper. Trim it if necessary. Reserve four apricot halves. Heat the oven to 375F (190C) gas 5.

Put the remaining apricots into a liquidiser or food processor together with their syrup, the herbs, mustard powder, soy sauce, yoghurt, lemon rind and half the breadcrumbs. Season and work them to a smooth sauce.

Put the liver into a baking dish, pour the sauce over it and cover it with foil. Bake it for 45 minutes. Remove the foil. Sprinkle the cheese and then the remaining breadcrumbs over the top. Bake for a further 15 minutes or until the top is crispy. While the liver is cooking, boil the rice until tender, about 15 minutes, drain it, rinse it with hot water and drain again. Fry the onion in the oil. Boil the carrots and peas separately, until tender. Drain them. Mix the vegetables into the rice.

Arrange the rice on a warmed serving dish. Place the liver on top and spoon over a little of the sauce. Garnish with the parsley sprigs and reserved apricot halves.

Serve the remainder of the sauce separately.

Muriel A. Constable, Blacon, Chester.

Turkey liver gougère

choux paste

2 oz (50 g) Cookeen or lard plus extra for greasing

¼ pint (150 ml) water

4 oz (125 g) flour

4 oz (125 g) Farmhouse Cheddar cheese, grated

2 eggs, beaten

filling

8 oz (225 g) turkey livers

2 tablespoons (30 ml) flour

4 oz (125 g) streaky bacon

1 oz (25 g) Cookeen or lard

2 medium onions, thinly sliced

3 tomatoes, scalded, skinned and chopped

4 tablespoons (60 ml) sherry

½ pint (275 ml) stock

Salt and pepper

Heat the oven to 400F (200C) gas 6. For the choux paste, put the fat and water into a saucepan and bring them to the boil. Take the pan from the heat and stir in the flour. Beat well and stir in the cheese. Cool the mixture and gradually beat in the eggs. Spread the paste in a ring round a greased 2-pint (1.15 litres) shallow, ovenproof dish. Bake it for 25 minutes or until golden brown and risen.

For the filling, trim and chop the turkey livers and toss them in the flour. Chop the bacon. Melt the fat in a frying pan on a low heat. Put in the onions and soften them. Add the liver, bacon, tomatoes, sherry and stock. Season. Cook them gently for 5 minutes.

Take the choux base from the oven and pile the turkey mixture into the centre. Reduce the oven to 325F (170C) gas 3 and return the dish to the oven for 15 minutes. Serve hot.

Serve with 2 lb (900 g) early purple sprouting, boiled for 6 minutes and drained, or *Turnips with orange* page 78.

Mrs M. Sponar, Heacham, Norfolk.

Kidney and lemon rice

1½ lb (675 g) ox or pig's kidney
4 tablespoons (60 ml) oil
About ½ pint (275 ml) water
1 teaspoon (5 ml) ground nutmeg
Salt and pepper
1 medium onion, sliced into rings
1 green pepper, sliced into rings
8 oz (225 g) mushrooms, thinly sliced
2 tablespoons (30 ml) tomato purée
6 oz (175 g) long grain white rice
Juice 1 lemon
Pinch ground turmeric

Cut the kidneys in half and cut out the cores. Slice the kidneys. Heat the oil in a frying pan on a medium heat. Put in the kidneys and brown them lightly. Remove them to a saucepan. Add enough water to cover them and season with the nutmeg, salt and pepper. Simmer them for 45 minutes, or until tender.

Gently fry the onion, pepper and mushrooms in the same oil until the onion is transparent. Add them to the kidneys. Stir in the tomato purée and simmer for 5 minutes.

Cook the rice in lightly-salted boiling water for 15 minutes, or until tender. Drain it well. Return it to the saucepan and set it on a low heat. Mix in the lemon juice and turmeric and heat through.

Arrange the rice on a warmed serving dish and spoon the kidneys on top.

Mrs J. L. Bacon, Westone, Northampton.

Bacon and mushroom lasagne

1 lb (450 g) good quality bacon pieces
1 onion, finely chopped
5 oz (125 g) mushrooms, thinly sliced
One 14 oz (400 g) tin tomatoes
4 tablespoons (60 ml) tomato purée
Salt and pepper
1 bayleaf
1 teaspoon (5 ml) Bisto
12 oz (350 g) lasagne
1 pint (575 ml) milk
1 oz (25 g) margarine
1 oz (125 g) flour
4 oz (125 g) Cheddar cheese, grated

Heat the oven to 350F (180C) gas 4. Chop the bacon, discarding the rind. Put it into a large saucepan and set it on a low heat. Cook it gently, stirring occasionally, until golden and crispy. Add the onion and cook until it is transparent, about 2 minutes. Add the mushrooms, tomatoes and tomato purée. Season well and put in the bayleaf. Dissolve the Bisto in 4 tablespoons (60 ml) water. Add it to the saucepan and stir until the mixture thickens. Cook it gently for 5 minutes, then remove the pan from the heat.

Cook the lasagne for 10 minutes in lightly-salted boiling water to which you have added 1 tablespoon (15 ml) oil. Drain it.

Melt the margarine in a saucepan on a low heat. Stir in the flour. Take the pan from the heat and stir in the milk. Bring the sauce to the boil, stirring. Take the pan from the heat and beat in the cheese. The sauce will be quite thin.

In a 9-inch (23 cm) square, ovenproof dish, layer the bacon mixture, lasagne and cheese sauce. The second layer of lasagne should be at right angles to the first. Finish with cheese sauce.

Bake the lasagne for 30 minutes, until the top is golden and bubbling.

Mrs J. E. Porter, Reading, Berks.

Stuffed cabbage rolls

8 large cabbage leaves
6 oz (175 g) brown rice
3 tablespoons (45 ml) oil
4 oz (125 g) onions, thinly sliced
4 chicken wings
¼ pint (150 ml) water
¾ oz (20 g) fresh root ginger, peeled and grated

gravy

1 tablespoon (15 ml) miso
½ pint (275 ml) water
1 teaspoon (5 ml) chopped thyme

Heat the oven to 325F (170C) gas 3. Parboil the cabbage leaves in lightly-salted water for 2 minutes. Drain them and cut away any tough stems. Simmer the rice, covered, in ¾ pint (425 ml) water for 45 minutes or until tender and all the water is absorbed.

Heat the oil in a frying pan on a low heat. Put in the onions and chicken wings and cook until both are lightly browned. Add the water and simmer for 20 minutes or until the chicken is cooked through. Cool in the pan. Skin the chicken wings, remove the meat and finely chop it.

Mix together the chicken, onion, ginger and rice. Divide the mixture between the cabbage leaves, putting it at the stalk end. Roll over the stalk end, fold in the sides and continue rolling up the leaf. Put the stuffed leaves into a shallow baking dish.

To make the gravy, gradually stir the water into the miso. Add the thyme. Pour the gravy over the cabbage rolls. Bake the rolls for 30 minutes, checking occasionally to make sure that the gravy does not become absorbed. If this happens, top up with hot water.

Serve with 1 lb (450 g) broccoli, steamed until tender and 1 lb (450 g) beetroot, boiled, sliced and served hot, sprinkled with 1 teaspoon (5 ml) dill seeds.

Editor's note: Miso is a thick, dark brown, savoury paste made from fermented soya beans, available in health food shops.

Janet Daly, Cardiff.

Chilli crêpes baked in cheese sauce

crêpes

8 oz (225 g) wholemeal flour
Pinch salt
2 eggs
1 pint (575 ml) milk
Oil for frying

filling

4 tablespoons (60 ml) oil
3 large onions, finely chopped
2 garlic cloves, finely chopped
3 celery sticks, finely chopped
8 oz (225 g) red kidney beans, soaked and cooked until tender
Two 14 oz (400 g) tins tomatoes; or 1½ lb (675 g) fresh tomatoes, scalded, skinned and chopped
10 oz (300 g) sweetcorn kernels, tinned or frozen
1 tablespoon (15 ml) tomato purée
1–2 tablespoons (15–30 ml) chilli powder

sauce

1 oz (25 g) butter
2 tablespoons (30 ml) wholemeal flour
½ pint (275 ml) milk
3 oz (75 g) Cheddar cheese, grated

For the batter, put the flour and salt into a bowl. Make a well in the centre and beat in the eggs and milk. Leave the batter to stand for 30 minutes in a cool place, and then use it to make sixteen pancakes.

For the filling, heat the oil in a saucepan on a low heat. Put in the onions, garlic and celery and soften them. Stir in the remaining ingredients and simmer, uncovered, until the mixture is thick, about 30 minutes.

For the sauce, melt the butter in a saucepan on a low heat. Stir in the flour and milk. Bring them to the boil, stirring, and stir until the sauce is thick. Take the pan from the heat and beat in the cheese.

Heat the oven to 375F (190C) gas 5. Put a tablespoon of the filling on to each pancake and fold the pancake like an envelope. Place the finished envelopes in a shallow baking dish and top them with the cheese sauce. Bake for 30 minutes or until browned.

Serve with *Spinach salad with celery seed dressing* page 82.

Mrs Syrel Dawson, London SW19.

Vegetable lasagne

1 lb (450 g) carrots
8 oz (225 g) mushrooms
One 14 oz (400 g) tin tomatoes
2 tablespoons (30 g) tomato purée
6 fl oz (175 ml) warm water
4 oz (125 g) margarine
1 large onion, finely chopped
3 garlic cloves, finely chopped
¼ teaspoon (1.5 ml) dried basil
Salt and freshly-ground black pepper
8 oz (225 g) lasagne verdi
2 oz (50 g) cornflour
½ pint (275 ml) milk
¾ oz (20 g) grated Parmesan cheese

Heat the oven to 350F (180C) gas 4. Finely peel and grate the carrots. Finely chop the mushrooms. In a bowl, break up and mash the tomatoes. Mix together the tomato purée and water.

Melt 1 oz (25 g) of the margarine in a saucepan on a low heat. Add the onion and garlic and soften them. Stir in the carrots and mushrooms and cook for a further 5 minutes. Add the tomatoes, thinned tomato purée, basil and seasonings. Remove from the heat.

Boil the lasagne verdi in lightly-salted water until tender, about 15 minutes. Drain it and cool it.

Melt the remaining margarine in a saucepan on a low heat. Stir in the cornflour and cook for 1 minute, stirring. Take the pan from the heat and gradually stir in the milk. Set the pan back on the heat and stir until the sauce boils and thickens. If it becomes too thick, stir in a little water 2 tablespoons (30 ml) at a time. Take the pan from the heat again and beat in half the cheese.

Layer the vegetable mixture, lasagne and sauce in a large casserole, in that order, ending with the vegetable mixture. Scatter the remaining cheese over the top. Bake the lasagne for 30 minutes.

Serve with *Lettuce and cucumber salad* page 82.

Janet Skea, London SW1.

Rice and lentils with tomato sauce

| 8 oz (225 g) split red lentils |
| 2 tablespoons (30 ml) oil |
| Salt and pepper |
| 1¼ pints (725 ml) stock (recommend Oxo cube) |
| 10 oz (300 g) brown rice |

| *sauce* |
| Two 14 oz (400 g) tins tomatoes |
| 1 green pepper, cut into strips |
| 2 tablespoons (30 ml) chopped celery leaves |
| ½ teaspoon (2.5 ml) salt |
| 1½ teaspoons (7.5 ml) ground cumin |
| Chilli powder to taste (recommend ¾ teaspoon (3.5 ml)) |

In a saucepan, gently fry the lentils in the oil for 5 minutes, stirring frequently. Season well. Pour in half the stock and cook gently for 10 minutes. Add the rice and remaining stock. Cook, covered, for 45 minutes, stirring several times to prevent sticking. It may be necessary to add a little more water. The final consistency should pour but be quite thick.

To make the sauce, put all the ingredients into a saucepan. Bring them to the boil and simmer for 20–30 minutes.

To serve, put the rice and lentils on to four plates and spoon the sauce over the top.

Serve with three large onions, thinly sliced and fried with four garlic cloves in 2 tablespoons (30 ml) oil until brown; and a green salad made with one lettuce, one cucumber and a handful of chopped fresh herbs such as sorrel, chives and parsley and dressed with ¼ pint (150 ml) natural yoghurt, preferably home-made.

Jenny Buels, Llanllechid, Gwynedd.

Corn and peanut flan

6 oz (165 g) flour
Salt and pepper
3 oz (75 g) margarine (not soft)
3 oz (75 g) Cheddar cheese, grated
2 tablespoons (30 ml) water
5 oz (150 g) salted peanuts
1 large carrot
6 oz (175 g) streaky bacon
One 12 oz (350 g) tin of sweetcorn, drained
3 eggs
1 egg yolk
3 tablespoons (45 ml) tomato ketchup
½ pint (275 ml) milk

Heat the oven to 400F (200C) gas 6. To make the pastry, sift and season the flour, rub in the margarine and stir in the cheese. Mix to a dough with the cold water. Roll out the dough and use it to line a 7 × 11 × 1-inch (18 × 26 × 2.5 cm) baking tin. Bake the pastry blind for 7 minutes

Turn the oven to 375F (190C) gas 5. Crush the peanuts in a plastic bag, using a rolling pin. Grate the carrot and chop the bacon. Mix together the nuts, carrot, bacon and sweetcorn. Put them into the pastry case, spreading them evenly. Whisk together the eggs, egg yolk, ketchup and milk. Pour the mixture into the flan.

Bake the flan for 30–40 minutes or until the filling is set. It can be served hot or cold.

Serve with a salad made from four large tomatoes, half a cucumber and 1 bunch watercress.

Louise Clark, Glasgow.

Vegetables and salads

Cabbage with tomatoes

8 oz (225 g) crisp white cabbage
One 14 oz (400 g) tin tomatoes
About 2 tablespoons (30 ml) oil
1 large onion, thinly sliced

Shred the cabbage. Drain and chop the tomatoes. Heat a heavy-based pan and put in just enough oil to coat the base. Put in the onion and stir until it is translucent, about 3 minutes. Add the cabbage and tomatoes. Stir well and season. Cover with a tight lid and turn the heat down low. Cook for 15 minutes.

Serve with *Orangey pork casserole* page 63.

Mrs Jill Kemp, Chester.

Calabrese au gratin

4 heads calabrese
2 tablespoons (30 ml) dry breadcrumbs
1 oz (25 g) Cheddar cheese, grated
1 oz (25 g) almonds, finely chopped

Trim the calabrese and cook it in lightly-salted boiling water for 10–15 minutes or until tender. Drain it well and put it into a heat-proof dish.

Mix together the breadcrumbs, cheese and almonds. Scatter them over the calabrese. Put the dish under a preheated high grill for about 2 minutes so the topping begins to brown.

Serve with *Stuffed spare rib pork chops* page 65.

Mrs Margaret Davies, London NW8.

Turnips with orange

2 lb (900 g) turnips
Grated rind and juice 1 medium orange
½ oz (15 g) butter

Peel and chop the turnips. Bring a pan of unsalted water to the boil and add the turnips and orange juice. Boil the turnips for 20 minutes or until tender. Drain them and put them into a heat-proof dish. Sprinkle them with the orange rind and dot with butter. Brown under a high grill.

Serve with *Turkey liver gougère* page 68.

Mrs M. Sponar, Heacham, Norfolk.

Oven cooked carrots

1 lb (450 g) carrots
1 tablespoon (15 ml) water
Salt
½ oz (15 g) butter
2 tablespoons (30 ml) chopped parsley

Heat the oven to 375F (190C) gas 5. Thinly slice the carrots and put them into an ovenproof dish. Add the water, season lightly with salt and dot with butter. Cover and cook in the oven for 1 hour. Serve straight from the dish, garnished with the parsley.

Serve with *Stuffed spare rib pork chops* page 65.

Mrs Margaret Davies, London NW8.

Glazed onions

1 lb (450 g) medium onions, peeled, left whole
1 oz (25 g) butter
1 teaspoon (5 ml) caster sugar
Salt and pepper

Drop the onions into lightly-salted boiling water. Cook them for 5 minutes and drain them well. Melt the butter in a saucepan on a low heat. Put in the onions, scatter in the sugar and season. Cover and cook very gently until the onions are tender and well glazed, about 20 minutes. Shake the pan from time to time and turn the onions, being careful not to let the sugar burn.

Serve with *Smoked haddock with brown rice* page 58.

Mrs E. R. I. Hanning, Newbury, Berks.

Potatoes with mint butter

4 baking potatoes, or 2 lb (900 g) new potatoes
4 oz (125 g) butter, at room temperature
4 oz (125 g) chopped mint

Beat the butter to a cream and beat in the mint. Form the butter into a roll or press it into a dish. Chill it in the refrigerator for 1 hour.

Bake the large potatoes in their jackets; or scrub and boil the new potatoes. Serve the butter separately.

Serve with *Smoked haddock roulade* page 59.

Mrs E. M. Monckton, Wrington, Avon.

Baked potatoes with coriander

4 large baking potatoes
1 oz (25 g) butter
6 tablespoons (90 ml) milk
2 teaspoons (10 ml) coriander seeds, toasted and crushed
Salt and pepper

Scrub the potatoes and prick them on both sides with a fork. Bake them in a preheated 400F (200C) gas 6 oven for 1 hour 30 minutes.

Cut each potato in half. Scoop out the pulp and mash it with the butter and milk. Season and mix in half the coriander. Pile the mixture back into the half shells and scatter the remaining coriander over the top. Put the potato halves on to a heatproof dish and put them back into the oven for 10 minutes to warm through.

Serve with *Avocado creamed chicken* page 60.

Maralyn Heathcock, Hagley, West Midlands.

Coleslaw

½ small white cabbage, shredded
1 medium carrot, shredded
1 medium onion, finely chopped
2 oz (50 g) sultanas
1 oz (25 g) sunflower seeds, toasted
dressing
4 oz (125 g) curd cheese
Approximately 6 tablespoons (90 ml) skimmed milk
Salt and freshly-ground black pepper
¼ teaspoon (1.5 ml) mustard powder

In a salad bowl, mix together the cabbage, carrot, onion, sultanas and sunflower seeds.

To make the dressing, beat enough skimmed milk into the cheese to give it a mayonnaise-like consistency. Season with the salt, pepper and mustard powder. Fold the dressing into the salad.

Serve with *Avocado creamed chicken* page 60.

Contributor's note: The dressing should be used on the day it is made as it becomes rather dry if left in the refrigerator overnight.

Maralyn Heathcock, Hagley, West Midlands.

Lettuce and caper salad

1 lettuce
¼ pint (150 ml) natural yoghurt
2 teaspoons (10 ml) capers

Wash and dry the lettuce and tear the leaves into small pieces. Place them on a flat dish. Pour the yoghurt over the lettuce and sprinkle the capers on top.

Serve with *Fish mollie with rice* page 57.

Patsy Nightingale, London N4.

Lettuce and cucumber salad

1 lettuce
½ cucumber
6 spring onions
Salt and freshly-ground black pepper
Juice ½ lemon

Wash and drain the lettuce. Tear the leaves into small pieces. Thinly slice the unpeeled cucumber. Chop the spring onions.

Put the cucumber and onions into a salad bowl. Season and add the lemon juice. Mix well, then toss in the lettuce.

Serve with *Vegetable lasagne* page 74.

Janet Skea, London SW1.

Spinach salad with celery seed dressing

1 lb (450 g) fresh spinach
4 oz (125 g) button mushrooms
1 small red onion
2 eggs, hard-boiled
4 fl oz (125 ml) oil
4 tablespoons (60 ml) white wine vinegar
1 tablespoon (15 ml) honey
½ teaspoon (2.5 ml) celery seeds
1½ teaspoons (7.5 ml) salt

Wash the spinach and cut off the tough stems. Tear the leaves into bite-sized pieces. Thinly slice the mushrooms and onion. Roughly chop the eggs. Mix these in a salad bowl.

Beat together the remaining ingredients and toss them into the salad.

Serve with *Chilli crêpes in cheese sauce* page 72.

Mrs Syrel Dawson, London SW19.

Salad platter

4 tablespoons (60 ml) oil
2 tablespoons (30 ml) white wine vinegar
Salt and pepper
½ lettuce
2 oz (50 g) frozen peas, cooked
2 oz (50 g) frozen sweetcorn, cooked
1 tablespoon (15 ml) chopped chives
¼ cucumber, unpeeled, diced
½ medium green pepper, deseeded and chopped
2 sticks celery, chopped
6 oz (175 g) carrots, grated
1 oz (25 g) sultanas
1 oz (25 g) red kidney beans, soaked and cooked
2 oz (50 g) French beans, broken into 1 inch (2.5 cm) lengths and cooked
2 oz (50 g) broad beans, fresh or frozen, cooked
2 tablespoons (30 ml) chopped parsley
½ box salad cress
¼ pint (150 ml) mayonnaise

Make the dressing by beating together the oil, vinegar and seasonings. Cover a flat serving dish with lettuce leaves.

First mix together the peas, sweetcorn and chives. Next mix the cucumber, celery and pepper and half the dressing; then the carrots and sultanas; and finally the red, French and broad beans with the remaining dressing.

Arrange the carrot salad across the centre of the serving plate and scatter the parsley over the top. Put the cucumber salad on one side and the bean salad on the other. Put a portion of the pea and corn salad on either end of the dish.

Garnish with the salad cress and serve the mayonnaise separately.

Serve with *Assisi chicken* page 62.

Mrs Vivienne Wayman, Stanmore, Middlesex.

Desserts

Apple crunch

1½ lb (675 g) cooking apples
2 oz (50 g) flour
5 oz (150 g) barbados sugar
3 oz (75 g) porridge oat flakes
4 oz (125 g) vegetable margarine

Heat the oven to 350F (180C) gas 4. Peel, core and slice the apples and put them into a baking dish. Mix together the dry ingredients and rub in the margarine as for a normal crumble. Top the apples with the mixture. Bake the crumble for 40 minutes or until the top is brown and the apples tender.

Mrs Syrel Dawson, London SW19.

Hazelnut apples

4 medium cooking apples
2 oz (50 g) shelled hazelnuts
1 oz (25 g) soft brown sugar
2 oz (50 g) unsalted butter, softened
2 egg whites
2 oz (50 g) caster sugar

Heat the oven to 375F (190C) gas 5. Peel and core the apples. Put them into cold, salted water until needed. Roast the hazelnuts for 10 minutes. Cool them and grind them in a blender or food processor; or put them into a greaseproof bag and crush them with a rolling pin. Mix the nuts with the sugar and butter.

Put the apples on to a heatproof dish and stuff them with the hazelnut mixture. Bake them, basting occasionally, for 20 minutes, or until beginning to soften.

Stiffly whip the egg whites and fold in the caster sugar. Spoon the meringue mixture over the apples and return the dish to the oven for it to brown, about 15 minutes. Serve hot.

Mrs B. Ferguson, Bridgwater, Somerset.

Chocolate pears

4 ripe pears
½ oz (15 g) shelled walnuts
½ oz (15 g) glacé cherries
¼ pint (150 ml) whipping cream, whipped
4 oz (125 g) dark chocolate
4 tablespoons (60 ml) cold black coffee
1 oz (25 g) margarine
2 eggs, separated

decoration

½ oz (15 g) angelica
Chopped nuts, or Jordans Original Crunchy Cereal, or Grapenuts

Very thinly peel the pears and core them. Finely chop the walnuts and cherries and mix them with 2 tablespoons (30 ml) of the whipped cream. Stuff the pears with the mixture.

Break up the chocolate and put it into a bowl with the coffee. Stand the bowl over a saucepan of simmering water and stir until the chocolate has melted. Take the bowl from the heat. Stir in the margarine and beat in the egg yolks. Whisk the egg whites until stiff and fold them into the chocolate mixture to give a mousse-like consistency. Pour the mixture over the pears to coat them.

Soften the angelica in warm water and cut it into leaf shapes. Press one on either side at the top of each pear. Chill the pears for at least 2–3 hours.

Just before serving, decorate the pears with the remaining whipped cream and scatter either chopped nuts, Jordans Original Crunchy Cereal or Grapenuts over the top.

Mrs J. L. Bacon, Westone, Northampton.

Compôte of rhubarb with baked egg custard and home-made yoghurt

1½ lb (675 g) rhubarb
Grated rind and juice 1 medium orange
3 oz (75 g) demerara sugar
2 eggs
1 oz (25 g) sugar
2 pints (575 ml) milk
1 tablespoon (15 ml) natural yoghurt

First make the yoghurt. Bring 1 pint milk to the boil, letting it rise in the pan. Draw it quickly from the heat and leave it to cool until you can hold your little finger in it for a count of 10, approximately 113F (45C).

Put the yoghurt into a bowl and stir in the milk. Cover and put the bowl into the airing cupboard. Surround it with a towel and leave it for 8 hours. If there is any liquid on the top, drain it off. Refrigerate the yoghurt before serving.

Trim and wipe the rhubarb and cut it into 1-inch (2.5 cm) lengths. Make the juice of the orange up to 1 pint (575 ml) with cold water. Put it into a large saucepan with the orange rind. Add the demerara sugar and stir on a low heat for it to dissolve. Bring to the boil and boil for 4 minutes or until you have a light syrup.

Put in the rhubarb and slowly bring the syrup back to the boil. Cook on a very low heat until the rhubarb is tender but the pieces still whole, about 15 minutes. Cool the compôte and then pour it into a glass, or other attractive, bowl.

For the custard, heat the oven to 300F (160C) gas 2. Beat the eggs with the sugar. Warm 1 pint of milk and stir it into the eggs. Strain the mixture into a buttered baking dish and bake for 50 minutes or until set. Serve warm. Serve the egg custard and yoghurt separately.

Mrs E. R. I. Hanning, Newbury, Berks.

Rhubarb and orange fool

1 lb (450 g) rhubarb
2 large oranges
6 oz (175 g) sugar
4 tablespoons (60 ml) water
½ oz (15 g) cornflour
½ pint (275 ml) milk
1 egg, beaten
Few drops pink food colouring, optional
¼ pint (150 ml) imitation cream
¼ pint (150 ml) single cream

Chop the rhubarb. Thinly pare away and chop the rind of one of the oranges. Cut away the pith. Cut the rind and pith from the remaining orange. Chop both oranges.

Put the rhubarb, oranges, orange peel, 5 oz (150 g) sugar and the water into a saucepan. Cover and set them on a low heat. Cook until the rhubarb is soft, 15–20 minutes. Cool slightly.

In a bowl, mix the cornflour to a paste with a little of the milk. Heat the rest of the milk in a saucepan. Pour it into the cornflour mixture. Stir well and return the mixture to the pan. Boil for 3 minutes, stirring continuously. Take the pan from the heat and cool the mixture a little. Beat in the egg and the remaining sugar. Return the pan to a very low heat and stir for 2 minutes, without boiling.

Mix the custard into the rhubarb. Add the food colouring if required. Liquidise until smooth. Cool and refrigerate for 1 hour.

Stiffly whip the imitation cream and fold it into the fool. Serve the single cream separately.

Janet Skea, London SW1.

Grapefruit cups

2 pink-fleshed grapefruit
4 oz (125 g) black grapes
1 small orange
1 pear
Juice ½ lemon
1 tablespoon (15 ml) honey
2 tablespoons (30 ml) dry sherry

decoration

¼ pint (150 ml) whipping cream, whipped
2 tablespoons (30 ml) chopped nuts

Cut each grapefruit in half. Remove the flesh and reserve the shells. Cut the flesh from the skin and chop it into ¾-inch (2 cm) pieces. Halve and seed the grapes. Cut the peel and pith from the orange and cut the segments from the skin. Cut them into ¾-inch (2 cm) pieces. Quarter, core and chop the pear. Toss the pieces in lemon juice. Put the fruits into a bowl.

Mix together the honey and sherry. Fold them into the fruits and leave to marinate for several hours, stirring frequently.

Pile the fruits into the grapefruit shells. Decorate with the whipped cream and chopped nuts.

Jenny Buels, Llanllechid, Gwynedd.

Grapefruit mousse

1 oz (25 g) powdered gelatin
2 tablespoons (30 ml) water
4 oz (125 g) full fat soft cheese
1 egg, separated
2 tablespoons (30 ml) natural yoghurt
½ tin frozen concentrated grapefruit juice, thawed
1½ oz (40 g) caster sugar
4 mint sprigs

In a small bowl, soak the gelatin in the water. Beat the cheese to a cream. Beat in the egg yolk and then, gradually, the yoghurt and grapefruit juice. Dissolve the gelatin over a saucepan of hot water. Stir it into the cheese mixture. Stand the bowl in cold water to cool.

Stiffly whisk the egg white. Whisk in the sugar. Fold the egg white into the cheese mixture. Pour the mixture into four ramekin dishes or stem glasses and chill it until set, about 1 hour. Just before serving, garnish each mousse with a mint sprig.

Mrs Vivienne Wayman, Stanmore, Middlesex.

Lemon and grapefruit soufflé

2 lemons
1 grapefruit
2 teaspoons (10 ml) powdered gelatin
4 tablespoons (60 ml) water
2 eggs, separated
2 oz (50 g) caster sugar
6 fl oz (175 ml) evaporated milk, chilled in the refrigerator overnight
2 tablespoons (30 ml) chopped or flaked almonds
¼ pint whipping cream, or single cream

Squeeze the juice from the lemons. Cut the rind and pith from the grapefruit and dice the flesh. In a small pan, soak the gelatin in the water.

In a bowl, beat together the egg yolks, sugar and lemon juice. Stand the bowl over a saucepan of hot (not boiling) water and beat until thick. Beat the evaporated milk until it is stiff. Dissolve the gelatin on a low heat. Stiffly whip the egg whites.

Fold the milk, the gelatin and the grapefruit pieces into the egg yolk mixture. Finally fold in the egg whites.

Pour the mixture into either a prepared soufflé dish or into a large, shallow dish. Chill it in the refrigerator for 2 hours or until set. To serve, decorate with the almonds and either pipe whipped cream on top or serve single cream separately.

Editor's note: To prepare a soufflé dish, cut a piece of greaseproof paper double the height of the dish plus six inches (15 cm) and 3 inches (7.5 cm) longer than the circumference. Fold it in half and oil one side. Oil the dish. Tie the paper securely round the dish.

Mrs Margaret Davies, London NW8.

Lemon sorbet

¾ pint (425 ml) water
Grated rind and juice 3 lemons
4 oz (125 g) caster sugar
1 egg white

optional garnish

Fresh mint leaves or 1 lemon, thinly sliced

Put the water into a saucepan. Add the lemon rind and bring to the boil. Simmer gently for 10 minutes. Strain. Add the sugar, stir until it dissolves, and leave to cool. Add the lemon juice. Pour the liquid into a shallow container and freeze it for 1 hour or until it is just firm.

Turn the frozen liquid into a bowl. Stiffly whip the egg white and fold it into the liquid with a metal spoon. Return the sorbet to the freezer for 2 hours. Put it into the refrigerator for 1 hour before serving. Spoon it into chilled glass bowls and decorate either with mint leaves or lemon slices.

Mrs E. M. Monckton, Wrington, Avon.

Home-made ice-cream with hot strawberry sauce

¼ pint (150 ml) whipping cream
2 large macaroons
2 eggs, separated
4 oz (150 g) icing sugar
2 tablespoons (30 ml) Cointreau
Juice and grated rind ½ medium orange
½ oz (15 g) mixed shelled nuts, crushed
8 oz (225 g) fresh strawberries

Stiffly whip the cream. Crush the macaroons so they resemble breadcrumbs.

Beat together the egg yolks and half the icing sugar until the mixture is frothy. This is best done by standing the bowl in a container of water. Whisk the egg whites until stiff and very slowly whisk in the remaining icing sugar. Fold in the egg yolks and mix in the macaroons, Cointreau and orange juice.

Pour the mixture into a spring-clip tin and sprinkle the nuts and orange rind over the top. Freeze quickly.

To turn out the ice-cream, wet a tea towel in hot water. Wrap it around the tin for a few moments and then release the spring-clip. Lift away the sides of the tin but leave the ice-cream on the base.

For the sauce, liquidise the strawberries in a blender or food processor; or rub them through a sieve. Heat the purée through just before serving, making sure it is very hot. Serve it separately to pour over the ice-cream like a sauce.

Patsy Nightingale, London N4.

Minty chocolate ice

5½ oz (165 g) dark cooking chocolate
One 14 oz (400 g) tin evaporated milk, chilled overnight in the refrigerator
1 teaspoon (5 ml) peppermint essence
1 egg white
4 mint sprigs

Melt the chocolate with 3 tablespoons (45 ml) of the evaporated milk and allow it to cool. Add the peppermint essence.

Whisk the chilled milk with an electric whisk until it is frothy and thick. Whisk in the chocolate mixture. Whisk the egg white until it is stiff and fold it into the rest.

Put the mixture into a shallow container and freeze it for at least 3 hours or overnight. Take it out of the freezer 10 minutes before serving.

Serve it in glass dishes, decorated with mint sprigs.

Contributor's note: This basic recipe can also be made into a fluffy mousse. Dissolve ½ sachet powdered gelatin in 1 tablespoon (15 ml) water over a low heat. Whisk it into the warm chocolate mixture before adding the milk. Continue to fold in the egg white. Pour the mixture into a dish and leave it in the refrigerator or in a cool place to set.

Louise Clark, Glasgow.

Apricot meringue with hot chocolate sauce

3 large egg whites
6 oz (175 g) caster sugar
1 teaspoon (5 ml) cornflour
1 teaspoon (5 ml) vinegar
½ pint (275 ml) double or whipping cream, whipped
1 oz (25 g) flaked almonds, lightly toasted
One 15 oz (425 g) tin apricot halves, drained

sauce
3 oz (75 g) cooking chocolate, broken
1½ tablespoons (20 ml) water
1½ oz (40 g) icing sugar
¾ oz (20 g) butter

Heat the oven to 300F (160C) gas 2. Line an 8-inch (20 cm) square tin with cooking parchment or oil it well. Stiffly whisk the egg whites. Mix together the sugar and cornflour and whisk them gently into the whites. Stir in the vinegar. Spread the mixture evenly in the prepared tin and bake it for 50 minutes or until set. Leave it for 5 minutes and then carefully turn it out on to a plate. Peel off the paper.

About 1 hour before serving, spread the cream over the meringue. Scatter the almonds round the edge and put the apricots in the centre.

Put the chocolate, water, icing sugar and butter into a bowl. Stand the bowl in a saucepan of simmering water and stir the ingredients with a wooden spoon to make a smooth sauce. Spoon the sauce over the apricot meringue just before serving.

Contributor's note: I always make my cream from 4 oz (125 g) unsalted butter and ¼ pint (150 ml) full cream milk, using a Bel cream maker.

Mrs Vivienne Wayman, Stanmore, Middlesex.

Walnut, lemon and apple meringue

crust

2 oz (50 g) shelled walnuts, chopped

3 oz (75 g) flour

2 oz (50 g) sugar

Grated rind ½ lemon

2 oz (50 g) butter, melted

1 egg yolk (size 3), beaten

filling

1 large Bramley apple

1 tablespoon (15 ml) lemon juice

2 tablespoons (30 ml) water

1 tablespoon (15 ml) soft brown sugar

1 egg yolk (size 3), beaten

1 oz (25 g) dry brown breadcrumbs

Grated rind ½ lemon

2 tablespoons (30 ml) lemon curd

meringue

2 egg whites (size 3)

4 oz (125 g) caster sugar

decoration

4 large walnut pieces

4 lemon slices

¼ pint (150 ml) whipping cream, whipped

Heat the oven to 375F (190C) gas 5. Lightly butter a 7-inch (18 cm) tart tin, or a 7-inch (18 cm) flan ring which is placed on a flat, heatproof plate. Mix together all the dry ingredients for the crust. Stir in the melted butter and egg yolk. Press the mixture into the base and sides of the prepared tin. Stand the tin on a baking sheet. Bake the crust blind for 25 minutes.

Peel, core and slice the apple. Put it into a saucepan with the lemon juice and water. Cover it and set it on a low heat for 15 minutes, or until it can be beaten to a fluffy purée. Take the pan from the heat and stir in the sugar and egg yolk.

Mix the breadcrumbs with the lemon rind and sprinkle them in the bottom of the crust. Warm the lemon curd and spread it over the breadcrumbs. Pile the apple mixture on top.

Stiffly whip the egg whites and whip in the caster sugar. Pile this meringue mixture on top of the apple, making it stand in peaks. Return the tart to the oven for about 20 minutes or until the meringue is crisp on top and lightly browned.

Decorate with the walnut pieces and lemon slices and serve the whipped cream separately.

Muriel A. Constable, Blacon, Chester.

Banana dacquoise

4 egg whites
8 oz (225 g) caster sugar
3 oz (75 g) ground almonds
Few drops almond essence
4 medium bananas
1 tablespoon (15 ml) lemon juice
4 fl oz (125 ml) whipping cream

Heat the oven to 275F (150C) gas 1. Line two baking trays with greaseproof or bakewell paper.

Stiffly whip the egg whites. Fold in the caster sugar and then the ground almonds and almond essence. Spread a 7-inch (18 cm) circle of the meringue mixture on each of the prepared baking trays. Bake the meringue bases for 1 hour, changing the position of the trays half-way through. Lift the lining papers complete with the meringues on to wire racks. When the meringues are cool, peel off the paper.

Mash the bananas with the lemon juice. Whip the cream and mix it into the bananas. Put one meringue circle on to a serving plate, spread it with the banana cream and top it with the second circle. Serve cold.

Mrs M. Sponar, Heacham, Norfolk.

Meringues with chestnut sauce and yoghurt

meringues

2 egg whites

3 oz (75 g) caster sugar

chestnut sauce

4 oz (125 g) dried chestnuts

4 oz (125 g) sugar

4 oz (125 g) powdered glucose

1 vanilla pod

7 fl oz (200 ml) water

for serving

1 pint (575 ml) natural yoghurt

To make the meringues, heat the oven to 225F (110C) gas ¼. Beat the egg whites until they stand in soft peaks. Add the sugar a little at a time, beating constantly until the mixture is smooth and thick. Drop the mixture in tablespoonfuls (15 ml spoons) on to a greased baking sheet. Bake them for 3 hours or until faintly tinged with colour.

For the sauce, soak the chestnuts for a few hours in cold water. Put them into a saucepan with fresh water and boil them until they are very soft and almost falling apart, about 1 hour. (If they are not absolutely soft they become hard when boiled with the sugar.)

Dissolve the sugar and glucose in the water. Bring them to the boil and boil fast for 5 minutes to obtain a syrup. Add the chestnuts and the vanilla pod. Simmer for about 20 minutes or until the mixture is thick. Remove the vanilla pod and let the mixture become quite cold.

Spoon the chestnut sauce into dishes and decorate it with the meringues. Serve the yoghurt separately.

Editor's note: Dried chestnuts can be bought in most wholefood shops and delicatessens. As an alternative, 12 oz (350 g) fresh chestnuts may be used. Skin them and boil in water to soften.

Janet Daly, Cardiff.

Special mince pie with sliced oranges

pastry
8 oz (225 g) flour
Pinch salt
Grated rind of ½ small orange and juice of one
2 oz (50 g) margarine
2 oz (50 g) lard
2 tablespoons (30 ml) milk
1 tablespoon (15 ml) icing sugar, sieved

filling
8 oz (225 g) mincemeat
4 oz (125 g) cream cheese
1 oz (25 g) caster sugar
4 small oranges
1 tablespoon (15 ml) liqueur (Cointreau or Grand Marnier if available)

First prepare the four oranges. Cut away the rind and pith and thinly slice the flesh. Put this into a dish and sprinkle with the liqueur. Cover them and chill them for several hours.

Heat the oven to 400F (200C) gas 6. Sift the flour with the salt. Add the orange rind and rub in the fats. Mix to a dough with the orange juice and extra water if needed.

Use half the pastry to line an 8-inch (20 cm) diameter pie plate. Spread the mincemeat over the pastry. Beat the cream cheese with the caster sugar and spread it over the mincemeat. Cover the pie with the remaining pastry and brush the top with milk.

Bake the pie for 10 minutes. Reduce the heat to 350F (180C) gas 4 and cook for a further 20 minutes, or until golden. Dust the pie with the icing sugar. Serve it warm, accompanied by the chilled oranges.

Jill Adams, Winchester, Hants.

Plum and almond tart

4 oz (125 g) flour
Pinch salt
2 oz (50 g) ground almonds
1 oz (25 g) icing sugar
2 oz (50 g) butter
1 egg yolk
2–3 tablespoons (30–45 ml) cold water
8 oz (225 g) plums
2 oz (50 g) shelled almonds, unblanched
3 oz demerara sugar

Heat the oven to 400F (200C) gas 6. For the pastry, sift the flour with the salt and stir in the icing sugar and ½ oz (15 g) of the ground almonds. Rub in the butter until the mixture resembles fine breadcrumbs. Bind to a dough with the egg yolk and a little water. Roll out the pastry and use it to line an 8-inch (20 cm) flan dish, fluting the edges.

Halve and stone the plums. Place the halves cut side down, in the flan case. Sliver the almonds and scatter them in between the plums. Sprinkle the demerara sugar and then the remaining ground almonds on top. Bake the tart for 30 minutes.

Contributor's note: Stoned prunes can be substituted for the plums.

Diana Jones, London N3.

Peanut pie

7 oz (200 g) digestive biscuits
4 oz (125 g) margarine, melted
One packet Dream Topping
3 oz (75 g) Philadelphia cream cheese
2 oz (50 g) icing sugar
1½ tablespoons (22.5 ml) peanut butter

Crush the biscuits and mix them with the melted margarine. Press the mixture into the base and sides of an 8-inch (20 cm) flan tin and leave it in a cool place for at least 1 hour to set.

Make up the Dream Topping according to the packet instructions. Beat the icing sugar and then the peanut butter into the cheese. Fold them into the Dream Topping. Spoon the mixture into the biscuit base and spread it evenly.

Refrigerate the pie for 24 hours before serving.

Mrs Margaret M. Pattison, London E11.

Curd cheesecake and cream

3 oz (75 g) digestive biscuits
2 oz (50 g) butter, melted
8 oz (225 g) curd cheese
2 eggs, beaten
2 oz (50 g) soft brown sugar
2 oz (50 g) sultanas
¼ pint (150 ml) single cream

Heat the oven to 400F (200C) gas 6. Crush the biscuits and mix them with the melted butter. Press the mixture into the sides and base of a 7-inch (18 cm) tart dish.

Beat the curd cheese to soften it. Gradually beat in the eggs. Fold in the sugar and sultanas. Pour the mixture into the biscuit base. Bake the tart for 30 minutes or until the filling is well-risen and brown.

Serve either warm or cold and serve the single cream separately.

Contributor's note: 4 tablespoons (60 ml) brandy or sherry or red wine flavoured with a pinch of ground cinnamon may be used instead of the butter.

Maralyn Heathcock, Hagley, West Midlands.